The Black History Bible How the Democrat Party Deceived a People

by Lisa Noel Babbage, PhD.

The Black History Bible
by Lisa Noel Babbage. PhD

Copyright 2020, Printed in the United States of America

ISBN-10 : 1796238902

ISBN-13 : 978-1796238907

All Rights Reserved.

Contents

Preface 6
The Hurt 8
Progress 9
A World at War 19
KKK & The Party 27
Democrat-dominated State Legislature 42
   JFK and the Democrats 60
Neo Liberalism 72
Black Power 93
Government Cheese 111
Gentrification 128
   Another change in policy 134
Gerrymandering 143
So Now, What? 162
The Healing 177
Who Can and Who Can't 178
  Who Can and Can't Vote in U.S. Elections
.... 178
    Who Can Vote? 178
    Who CAN'T Vote? 179

Your First Time? 180
   First Time Voters 180
   Exceptions to Voter Identification Requirements 180

Preamble Left 182

Preamble Right 189

Election Crimes 195

Accessibility in Voting 199

Absentee & Early Voting 201
   Absentee Voting 201
   Early Voting 202

Teaching Patriotism 204

The Whisper Room 210

About the Author 212

Also by Lisa Babbage 214

  333 Miracles A testimony of Continued Blessings 214

  Not So Cookie Cutter Kids 215

Preface

Over the years, Black History Month has come to be a source of pride for African-Americans from coast to coast. Yet in many communities, the myths surrounding our modern history is being skewed by media propaganda, special interest groups, and those attempting to cast a shadow on the progress we have made in this nation. Find out how scripture and history collide in this exposé into the Democrat Party in America.

The Black History Bible How the Democrat Party Deceived a People

The Hurt

Many black Americans have been hurt by our nation's past. Even our nation's present can be insulting, frustrating, and cumbersome. Regardless of how you feel about your neighbor, or yourself, you owe it to the future generations of little black girls and boys who will come after you face the truth about our political system. As Martin Luther King, Jr. often reminds us, you may never be President, but you can always be a king.

Progress

But they will progress no further, for their folly will be manifest to all, as theirs also was-
2 timothy 3:9

Photo Credit Jude Beck

It's all in a word — progress, a forward motion that is indicative of change that is lofty in some way, more ethereal in nature, and, of course, redemptive. Progress, progressives, and progressive reform is synonymous with the Democrat Party, and for good reason.

In recent history, President Woodrow Wilson, who took office in 1913, based his theories about how to run the country in socialism, which was considered by some to be a progressive reform. The former Governor of New Jersey called his presidential campaign the "New Freedom" which was in contrast and opposition to Roosevelt's "New Nationalism." According to research, had it not been for candidate Jennings Bryan support of Wilson as the Democratic nominee after a mob-based Tammany Hall boycott of moderate Democrats which opened the door for Wilson in the first place. Wilson is the early face of the Democrat Party.

According to the Miller Center, a political think tank who claims a nonpartisan affiliation with the University of Virginia,

Wilson is one of the America's greatest Presidents. Wilson's nickname, "Schoolmaster in Politics," does not reflect the actual legacy of the welfare state he so aptly promoted. Wilson's internationalism opposed the ideas behind nationalism, introduced the idea of global citizenry long before modern political conversations turned the idea of nationalism into a "dark and dirty suggestion" based in self-aggrandizing.

Wilson painted a picture of traditional American ideals as being self-centered, egotistical, and archaic. The nationalistic agenda was forced back during his administration, making way for the Democrat Party to be called the party of reform, i.e. progressive.

Your average American hears the word progressive and immediately decides it's a good thing. We rely on old adages like, "If you're not progressing, you're regressing." "If you're not first, you're last." Even catch phrases like "smarter, better, faster" give us the idea that being progressive is the end all, beat all goal. Wilson understood, or at least his political advisers understood, that public opinion is the way to shape policy, your constituency, the nation, and even the world. Under his leadership, Congress enacted the most cohesive, complete, and elaborate program of federal oversight of the nation's economy up to that time: banking reform under the auspices of the Federal Reserve System (Revenue Act of 1913 passed his first year in office), tariff reduction, federal regulation of business, support for labor and collective bargaining, and federal aid to education and agriculture. (Woodrow Wilson: Impact and Legacy, Saladin Ambar)

Yet in years since, including those years immediately following Wilson's last year in office, the country took a financial dive only a few eager millionaires could get us out of. 'New Freedom' became Wilson's domestic agenda. He implemented the income tax, which many reveal the IRS tax code does not mandate, neither does the Constitution. Wilson presided over the Federal Reserve

Act which brought us the IRS and a central banking system <u>not</u> based on free, competitive markets, but rather based on a private banking system run by elites. Raising the estate tax to penalize the wealthy and the antitrust laws to limit large corporations called trusts, Wilson's reforms broadened the scope of government immensely. Woodrow Wilson kept America neutral during World War I. In his second term, he expanded the military and proposed limits on working hours, by including the provision for a six-day working week and minimum wage. These were necessary reforms. Yet much of what Wilson aimed to do reached beyond the bounds of our Constitution in many ways. In 1917, Woodrow Wilson finally led America into World War I stating that Germany wanted "nothing less than war against the government and people of the United States," even though the Germans had ravaged Europe for years threatening global democracies and our Republic.

In a speech known as the Fourteen Points of Light, Wilson attempted to be the one leader who organized peace in the world. Some remark that Wilson's reluctance to join World War I were steeped in his idealized design to be seen as a peacekeeper. Wilson launched the League of Nations, which would later be replaced by the United Nations, as part of his 'One World Government' scheme.

Photo Credit Clem Onojeghuo

While the Democrat Party is one of the two major political parties in the United States, it is by far one of the nation's oldest existing political party being founded in 1828. After the Civil War, the party dominated in the South due to its opposition to civil and political rights for African Americans. After a major shift in the 20th century marketing,

today's Democrats are known for their association with a strong federal government and support for minority and women's rights, environmental protection and progressive reforms. Yet they still have a tether to African Americans; no longer on the leash of legal slavery. Now Democrats are inextricably linked to minorities through propagandizing the victim-hood mentality.

Photo Credit Vlad Tchompalov

Modern progress under the Democrat Party expanded definitions of marriage that included same-sex marriage, abortion on-demand, weakened international trade, loosened border security, proposed regulations on guns, increased social reparations through welfare and universal healthcare, and a liberal social platform. Some Americans, while giving credit to the Party for electing the nation's first African American President, felt the progressive tendencies in the name of progress under the Democrats have weakened the morality of the country. Centrists, part of the New

Democratic Coalition, called New Dems, are capitalists Democrats that favor balanced budgets, and moderate agendas based on the platform as a whole. Liberal leaning leftist progressives (of the Congressional Progressive Caucus) is a faction of the party itself, the faction that makes the most headlines.

Dixiecrats, southern Democrats, who did not favor the expansion of government under progressive democratic policies, including segregation, left the party temporarily, garnering a large number of black votes in the process. The History Channel states, "Most Dixiecrats returned to the Democratic fold, but the incident marked the beginning of a seismic shift in the party's demographics. At the same time, many black voters who had remained loyal to the Republican Party since the Civil War began voting Democratic during the Depression, and would continue to do so in greater numbers with the dawn of the civil rights movement." We live in a world where Dixiecrats and African American voters share a party of "progress." Progress, but toward what end?

The Bottom Line

- The Republican Party was created before the Civil War so that the sons and daughters of slaves could participate freely in government.
- Abraham Lincoln, the party's first president, swore an oath to lead the country into war, if necessary, to defeat slavery.

- Southern Democrats and racist northerners attempted to overthrow the government by succeeding from the Union in order to maintain the practice of slavery.
- Democrats benefited from social programs of the Great Depression age to pull black voters and poor whites to their political affiliation through welfare.
- After the Civil War, Southern Democrats known as Dixiecrats continued the aggression against blacks in America through strategic advertising within the Democrat Party.

A World at War

It was given power to wage war against God's holy people and to conquer them. And it was given authority over every tribe, people, language and nation.

~   Revelation 13:7

In 1920, the Democratic Convention opened in San Francisco with a speech by Homer Cummings, who honored second term President Woodrow Wilson as 'immortal' for his work with the Treaty of Versailles by saying, "In one sense it is quite immaterial what people say about the President. Nothing we can say can add or detract from the fame that will go down the unending channels of history."

This election, our eventual participation in World War I, and his domestic acts which contributed to President Franklin D. Roosevelt's New Deal caused Wilson to be seen as a hero, according to history books.

However, the business partnership between a private bank, deceivingly named the Federal Reserve, and the American government has received much criticism, especially in recent years. As the Federal

Reserve surpasses the legal boundaries it once expressed, it does so reminiscent of thug like tactics, wage garnishment, and interest rates that disproportionately penalize the lower middle class. To this day, the Federal Reserve Bank dominates the global financial industry. Wilson indebted this country to the Federal Reserve during World War I to the tune of billions of dollars. His administration took control of American railroads, demanded America fight for democracy in defunct European nations after the armistice despite obvious obstacles to implement, and he further expanded government at home. While Wilson received the Nobel Peace Prize for his role in the League of Nations, Congress never supported America's participation in the League and Wilson lost his re-election bid to a Republican candidate by a landslide.

While the League of Nations continued to extend influence around the globe, America continued to assert its power in the Western hemisphere, especially in Mexico. Before leaving office, President Wilson inserted American agendas in Mexico, Cuba, Haiti, Panama, the Dominican Republic, Nicaragua, and other areas of Latin America. In other words, Democrat President Woodrow Wilson injected American control into impoverished nations where blacks and Hispanics were the predominant population. America's influence in the region were seen as anti-Hispanic, corporate-driven for economic gain, and gave America control over foreign debt, sinking the United States further into economic compromise.

Peasant resistance in the Dominican, civil unrest in the Mexican Revolution, and the "Banana Wars" throughout Central and South America were all orchestrated for economic gains at the expense of the American taxpayers who were forced to finance Wilson's foreign policy. While Wilson was not the only president to lead America into conflict with Latin America, his administration exceeded the efforts of past presidents by expanding America's reach in the region and indebted our country in the process. Democrat Woodrow Wilson ignored many domestic challenges at home, in favor of attempting to expand

American influence in other nations with unstable governments. These are the practices that America is most criticized for globally. All the while, southern blacks were being discriminated against in a climate of systematic racism in Democratic-led cities. Wilson continued the cycle of funding the Central American region for political control there. However, the American influence never included sound policies that developed those nation's infrastructure or educational systems. The economies of these nations were never stabilized even after 100 years and billions of dollars later.

Most will be surprised that America once militarily occupied the Dominican Republic and handpicked Haiti's president after a long occupation there. Nicaragua avoided military occupation by the United States through "diplomacy" and was able to transfer their foreign debt to the United States while receiving 3 million in exchange for rights to build a canal and naval base in that country. The canal was never built after many failed attempts.

While Wilson's initial victory regarding Panama may have been a mute point if Theodore Roosevelt had not led a split to form an offshoot of the Republican party called The Progressives, Wilson narrowly won a second term in 1916. " During the late months of 1916 and the early part of 1917, The Outlook reflected the impatient spirit shown toward Wilson for his delay in severing relations with Germany. The chief value of these articles was "an illustration of the animosity toward Wilson, so noticeable in Congress and among the people," according to a 1936 thesis on Woodrow Wilson's relationship with the Democrat Party submitted to Loyola University Chicago. It continues, "Articles printed in The Metropolitan Magazine New York, 1917, illustrated the attack by Roosevelt against Wilson. Editorials, some the work of Roosevelt, appeared with startling frequency showing the tragedies of an ill conducted war, the need for war cabinet and the crime of lack of preparedness. The disapproval of Congressmen toward Wilson's war moves was eagerly recounted in these monthly issues."

The crime of unpreparedness is still being realized today. Because of the systems Wilson put in place: systems that still tie America to foreign debt in exchange for little more than foreign criticisms. These systems fail to provide actual stability in compromised regions and paved the way for militant rule by drug lords and paramilitary organizations which occupy until socialism or communism emerges in these nations.

In retrospect, Wilson capitalized on our world at war in the same way totalitarian regimes did in Europe, exploiting Latin American nations. He expanded the federal government in a way that has become indicative of the Democrat Party. Wilson's race reputation cast a shadow on American foreign policy, and while he is the father of modern liberalism, his civil liberties record pales in comparison with the claims modern Democrats support.

The Bottom Line

- Liberal policies infiltrated the White House with the election of Woodrow Wilson.
- American ideologies toward African Americans became increasingly less civil and more overt in developing a plan for systematic racism.
- The federal government ballooned under Democratic control in the early 1900's.
- Global wars that occurred after World War I were the excuse given by America and other nations for the creation of the League of Nations (precursor to the United Nations), which included only 2 free African nations in its membership at the onset. [Membership in the League of Nations was approximately 4% African voting power, 40% Hispanic nations, nearly 50 Anglo nations, and 6% Asian.]

KKK & The Party

Discipline your children, for in that there is hope; do not be a willing party to their death.
~ Proverbs 18:19

BASKETBALL GAME
KLU KLUX KLAN vs. KNIGHTS OF COLUMBUS
BENEFIT
JEWISH RELIEF ASSOCIATION
MASONIC AUDITORIUM

Sponsored by Advancement for Colored People

ST. PATRICK'S DAY - MARCH 17TH
BEER SERVED BY BAPTIST CHURCH
RUSSIAN REFEREES - ADMISSION: $1.00

Parody Ticket

Politifact.com asserts that it is not fair to say that the Democrat Party founded the Ku Klux Klan, a white supremacist group found primarily in the Southern United States. What they could confer is that many early Democrats used the Klan as their strong arm. Of course, as with any underground organization, there is no membership disclosure. Even the hooded marchers themselves disguise their racist identities in order to infiltrate mainstream organizations, even political organizations. In 1868, during future Democratic President Woodrow Wilson's impressionable youth, the Klan served as a major part of the Democrat Party, speaking at the National Convention and holding elected office. Klan members taunted their white might slogans at every turn, using tactics to legally bind blacks across Dixie. Klansmen even marched on Washington, routinely burning crosses, terrorizing citizens, and dividing the nation. The major theme of these the loudest voices in America yelled, "This is a White Man's Country, Let White Men Rule."

In 1872, during the next nationwide election cycle, the theme was "New Departure," a departure from the Republican reforms of Reconstruction and rebuilding the south after the Civil War. When Congress attempted to transform the war torn south, Democrat-led southern states reconciled themselves to political rhetoric since military manpower was not an option. In short, a different kind of fight to keep African-Americans enslaved was put into motion. The Klan played an active role in keeping freed blacks from voting, achieving economic advancement, or exercising any rights that our Constitution provided. In those days the Republican platform was called 'liberal' by Dixiecrats who saw the idea of making segregation illegal a progressive notion. Liberalism became synonymous with the Republicans efforts to end segregation in the south. The term liberal during this time in America's history bears little resemblance to the current definition, because the initial meaning was based on Constitutionality that was systematically deprived from black citizens by deep state racism in our nation, not an open invitation to redefine traditional norms.

A splinter group, who received less that one percent of the vote, called themselves the Straight Out Democrats, a conservative base that supported a Charles O'Connor/John Quincy Adams II ticket in the election cycle shortly after the Civil War. They held a national convention in Louisville, Kentucky, on the basis that any voter turnout would not result in electoral college votes because the Democratic National Committee did not recognize the Straight Out Democrats as an official political party. In other words, the few conservative Democrats that broke away from the racist policies of the party were politically ostracized for their conservative stance, and were largely unrecognized and legitimized by traditional Democrats. The Democrat Party during the Klan's infiltration into politics represents a truly liberal platform more representative of modern definitions.

The Republican party also experienced a split in 1872. The Liberal Republican Party nominee, Horace Greeley, a candidate who failed to secure the bid for the Republican nomination, became the Liberal Republican Party nominee for the presidency and was eventually supported by the Democrat Party within months of the election. While the Liberal Republican Party platform valued some of the same principles of their more conservative counterpart, such as matters concerning the equality of all men regardless of color, persuasion (whose broadest terms include matters of sexuality), religion, nativity or race, there was a debate about how matters of reconstruction would be carried out. In other words, there was a debate between this Republican splinter group and the Republicans of Lincoln as to how blacks would be compensated after slavery.

In just seven years after the Civil War, Democratic support of Horace Greeley to divide the chances of Republicans and the 1872 election ended poorly as the party who lost to Ulysses S. Grant's Republicans.

Their efforts to "remove the vestiges of Confederate nationalism, racism, and slavery" were seen as the best interest of the Union by the people who vastly voted for the war hero.

Greeley, who popularized the slogan, "Go West, young man, and grow up with the country," eventually served in Congress, representing New York; and continued to promote his ideas of feminism and socialism. Reconstructionist ideals in favor of reparations of the first two years of Grant's administration caused southern Democrats to rise up at the polls. In 1874, the policies of Grant's administration were called Pro-Black. Democrats exploited the inadequate implementation of these kinds of reconstruction policies as a failure of the administration and as a result (Democrats) took control of the House of Representatives. Democrats also had a majority in the Senate as a result of the criticisms of Grant's White House. This set in order the introduction of Jim Crow laws.

Democratic led House and Senate called for the removal of federal troops from southern states, leaving newly freed blacks to fend for themselves in post-Civil War America. State and local laws in Democratic-led state legislatures brought about radical change in the former Confederate States of America. Jim Crow, modeled partially after a caricature of a man in black face, kept black Americans oppressed, economically and socially, in a time when the country was trying to heal from the battles that killed a generation of soldiers. Jim Crow laws led to "separate but equal" racial segregation doctrines. The laws institutionalized economic, social, and educational disadvantages for non-white communities including poll taxes which kept blacks from exercising their rights to vote.

These decades of disenfranchisement of black communities was highlighted by racist leadership in the south. More famous, perhaps, than any other in this movement was Woodrow Wilson. His pattern of appointing Southern Democrats to his cabinet ensured the segregationist patterns that would become more and more commonplace, nationally, not just in the South. Wilson believed segregation was better for both African-Americans and what he called European-Americans, alike. The Great Reunion of 1913 was led by a spirit of white supremacy and the solid, systematic oppression of blacks in the south was embedded despite early attempts to quell Jim Crow segregation under Massachusetts Senator Charles Sumner's Republican leadership.

Republicans criticized Democrats for using "slave power" to influence the federal government even after the practice of slavery became illegal. For example, South Carolina Democratic Senator Andrew Butler was an avid proponent of slavery. His ties to the KKK were further evidenced by his families strong hold on Congress (a cousin, his brother, and nephew all served in the US Congress). The National Historic Registry application for the Butler Family Cemetery in South Carolina indicated Andrew Butler was a champion for nullification, urging states to choose rights for themselves despite the passing of the Reconstruction amendments which basically mandated the abolition of slavery and other rights concerning the descendants of slaves.

Like many southern states, North Carolina (Congressman Brooks, Governor Manning, and Judge Heyward), Georgia (Governors Cobb, Forsyth, Early, Telfair, Troup, Walton, Milledge, Colquitt, Crawford, and Senator Barrien), Alabama (Governors Watts and Bibb), South Carolina (Senator W. Hampton I, Judge Heyward, and Governor W. Hampton III), and Tennessee (Governor Houston), <u>all had Democratic leaders who were slave owners</u>. William Aiken, Jr., former Governor of South Carolina, for example, was considered one of the nine biggest slave owners in the Union. David Atchinson, a Freemason and acting Democratic President in 1849 was a slave owner and Klan supporter. Democratic President Andrew Jackson owned and traded slaves while in office and did not free them upon his death. Democratic President William Henry Harrison owned slaves, led a pro-slavery movement in the western territory, and fathered six children with one of his female slaves. Harrison's funeral procession was detailed in the memoir Twelve Years a Slave. James Polk, eleventh President of the United States, became the Democratic nominee for president in 1844 partially because of his tolerance of slavery, in contrast to former president and Democrat candidate Martin Van Buren, a man who was less vocal about slavery and did not support the annexation of Texas. For the first time in their history, Democrats united expansion-minded Northerners and racist southern Dems behind the issue of Texas.

James Polk generally supported slavery as president. His Last Will and Testament provided for the freeing of his slaves after the death of his wife, though the Emancipation Proclamation and the Thirteenth Amendment to the United States Constitution ended up freeing them long before her death in 1891, according to research. His strong stance on slavery was a selling point for the south, and his desire to see Texas enter into the Union bode well with many in the north.

Madison, the third President of the United States who was in office before the Democratic-Republicans split into two parties, proposed the three-fifths compromise stating that slave labor was a necessity to the southern economy. His private thoughts notwithstanding, Madison was a weak president on the issue of slavery. John Tyler, tenth President of the United States, a Democrat turned Whig, was a strong supporter of state's rights and believed and owned slaves. His goal was to regulate slavery as to tax it and allow it throughout the territory. All of these leaders had strong ties to slavery and the oppression of blacks, many even after the abolition of slavery. President Van Buren, the founder of the original Democrat Party, was a proponent of slavery even while in office. However, after his presidency he became more conservative regarding the institution and support Abraham Lincoln's petition to end slavery. Like abortion in today's political debate, slavery was the deciding factor between Democrats and Republicans in the early years of our nation.

Most wealthy landowning families in the new colonies and later in the states owned slaves. However, in the very early years of our nation, the abolitionist movement in the New England states had a great effect of gaining political favor. The country was soon divided on the issue of slavery, Republicans seeking to dissolve the practice, Democrats defending the practice. When the Civil War broke out, there were effectually no slaves in the Northern part of the country.

Looking back from Wilson to Reconstruction is important to demonstrate the lengthy relationship the Ku Klux Klan had with the Democrat Party. Eighteen Presidents, including George Washington, owned slaves. Even Abraham Lincoln's Vice President, Andrew Johnson, who assumed the presidency after his assassination, owned slaves. This is an odious part of America's history. However, northern Republicans changed their views on slavery when southern Democrats held firm to the cause of 'states rights,' which in effect was simply the right to own, buy and sell black slaves who were illegally imported into the country for nearly 100 years after we won our independence from England. According to the History Channel, "Such tendentious revisionism may provide a useful corrective to older enthusiastic assessments, but it fails to capture a larger historical tragedy: Jacksonian Democracy was an authentic democratic movement, dedicated to powerful, at times radical, egalitarian ideals — but mainly for white men." Slavery, the use of the Ku Klux Klan as a social restraint, political infiltration especially in the south, and economic and educative inferiority kept the sons and daughters of slaves, and former slaves, imprisoned. Jacksonian Democrats, those in office after 1829, did not want to upset the delicate balance of power among white men. They considered blacks, Hispanics, and Indians to be inferior peoples and favored establishing norms that would benefit poor whites over reconstruction ideas that benefited people of color.

Perhaps no one will ever be able to find the clear link of affiliation between early Democrats and the KKK, but the pattern of "if the shoe fits, wear it" is clear. These slave owners who did nothing to prohibit Klan activity. Instead they used their political power to oppress freed blacks and did little to promote the ideas of reconstruction in the south. In short, the only difference between Democrats and the Ku Klux Klan in the days after the Civil War was the costume they wore.

The Bottom Line

- The Klu Klux Klan is directly responsible for 3,500 black deaths.
- Margaret Sanger's eugenics movement is responsible for 19 million black deaths through Planned Parenthood.
- Black on black crime doubles the number of blacks killed, every year, by Dixiecrat Klansmen in 86 years.

- Blacks have been compromised economically through the practices of slave-owning Democrats in politics for over 100 years.
- Even after slavery was abolished, Democrats in power worked within the law to further economically enslave black people.

Democrat-dominated State Legislature

But that does not mean we want to dominate you by telling you how to put your faith into practice. We want to work together with you so you will be full of joy, for it is by your own faith that you stand firm.

~ 2 Corinthians 1:24

Before 1965, blacks in the South were at the mercy of a man they never met; a man named Jim. Jim Crow laws were enacted in the Democratic-dominated south as a way of extending the chains of slavery after the Emancipation Proclamation. In essence, the laws revolved around suppressing votes, intimidation tactics limiting the expression of free speech, Constitutional rights, and other provided for privileges granted to American citizens. Examples were well documented in the 2011 movie The Help. Many blacks in the south worked for menial wages, not minimum wage.

These men and women were guaranteed their citizenship as the sons and daughters of slaves who earned de facto birthright citizenship when President Lincoln signed the Emancipation Proclamation. Yet, they were routinely kept from their civil liberties, especially in the Democrat-dominated south. Men were regularly kept from promotions in the workplace and obviously the school systems were disadvantaged. Many black teens dropped out of school early to add to the financial support to their families. In other words, blacks were placed in economic slavery because our federal government made physical slavery illegal but failed to protect blacks from power hungry Democrats, especially in the South.

Jim Crow laws created or at least propagated a slavery mentality toward black populations. To put it briefly, Jim Crow is a type of "separate, but equal" doctrine. This idea created an even bigger division between ethnicity in America. Why was Jim Crow so significant? The simple answer is its "subtle-ness." Starting in the 1870's, after the Civil War, Democrats who lost on the battlefield began part two of their plan to keep people entitled to a free market society functionally enslaved. Logistically this may have been carried out in any number of ways. The Constitution stated that black Americans, just like white Americans, had the right to vote. Local municipalities might pass a local law or ordinance to add a poll tax in every election that would have been cost prohibitive for someone making a meaniel wage would not be able to afford. From additional local taxes or fees to mandatory applications to exercise constitutional rights, local Democrats effectively kept free blacks "in their place."

According to reports "as a body of law, Jim Crow institutionalized economic, educational, and social disadvantages for African Americans, and other people of color living in the south. Legalized racial segregation principally existed in the Southern states, while Northern and Western racial segregation generally was a matter of fact—enforced in housing with private covenants in leases, bank lending-practices, and employment-preference discrimination, including labor-union practices."

Actions against restricted civil rights and civil liberties were the basis of the Civil Rights movement of the 1960's. Roughly 100 years after Black Codes, like Jim Crow, passed in southern states which were aimed at keeping a population enslaved, the Civil Rights Movement sought to undo what was allowed the Democratic-led legislature in many southern states. Black codes', also called Slave Codes, unspoken goal was to decrease or eliminate the influence of blacks politically and economically. This is meant not only to eliminate influence in the polling place, but also in neighborhoods, communities, and even families.

Black males, for example, were constantly demeaned by whites, male and females, in public and private institutions. The term "boy" being applied to grown men, for example, undermined the natural hierarchy of order in the home. This process of targeting of a particular "minority" group and demeaning the natural maturation and stabilization of those families was done under the leadership of Democrat legislators. Frankly, it is still happening today but the tactics are even more subtle. Mass marketing that promotes victimization and victim mentality among blacks or other persons of color promotes fear and anxiety.

In the past, bigoted legislators who were opposed by negro leaders and Republicans, modeled the state laws passed in their chambers on slavery itself; regulating gun ownership, meeting for worship, learning to read and write, and other constitutional rights to movement and labor. Although some northern states had similar laws during slavery, those laws were repealed when slavery was abolished after the Civil War. Now the modelling takes on similarities to socialism and propagandized techniques which circumvent the Constitution. The theory of "blacks and browns" as a singular people group is another example of modern propaganda that marginalizes African Americans. Most "browns" for instance, are immigrants who speak two or three languages, are incentivized to come to America, and can "skip the line" on economic opportunity as first generation immigrants. They have no emotional or economical scarring as a result of slavery. They have no mental affiliation or emotional reaction to words like "boy," "negro," or a white face. On the contrary, many "browns" who immigrate to America consider themselves of a higher socio-economic standard than black people born in this country.

Elected southerners in the Democrat Party also contributed to expanded vagrancy laws that forced those who were found guilty of minor infractions, such as jaywalking, were forced into involuntary labor to pay for the debt they incurred as a result of their "crime." This is very similar to the extended probation and parole monitoring practices that plague urban communities today. People who are now kept on punitive probation for non-violent crimes due to their inability to pay exorbitant fines are a byproduct of the Jim Crow or Slave Codes of the past.

By current estimates, most counties in the south that have extensive numbers of persons on probation. In Georgia there are close to one million people on monitoring programs such as probation, which is commensurate to the way blacks were discriminated against right after the Civil War. Being perceived as a dangerous social problem after the war, blacks were made to be held responsible for the loss and devastation that occurred in the south. In other words, white democrats who lost money in the war, lost their right to a free labor force and a host of other economic advantages, felt the need to impose state-level laws that would allow them to recoup the expense they spent on fighting a losing cause. The term 'super-predator,' 'repeat offender,' and other 'three strikes' crackdowns implicitly targeted people who live in urban areas; i.e., Blacks.

But what does this all add up to? When Republican (National Union Party was the name used during the Civil War) Abraham Lincoln signed the document freeing the slave population in American, rich southerners, who were by far predominantly democrat, organized the KKK and passed discriminatory laws called Jim Crow laws in an attempt to recover the traditions of slavery. Through domestic terrorists like the Klan, morally corrupt legislation, a propaganda movement of racism, and numerous other legal and illegal measures, southern Democrats promoted economic, educational, and other disparages among black citizens. In many ways, they still do today.

Of the twelve states in the southeast (Georgia, South Carolina, Alabama, Kentucky, Virginia, West Virginia, Mississippi, Arkansas, Florida, Tennessee, and Louisiana), the majority of them have had Democratic leadership since Jim Crow laws were instituted. For example, Alabama had a Democratic governor from 1826 to 2002, except for a few years here and there when an independent, Whig, or Republican was in office for one term. That equates to 100 years of Democrat rule, and Alabama ranks as one of the worst economies in the United States according to a 2016 poll.[1]

1

https://www.al.com/news/2016/06/new_study_finds_alabamas_econo.html

Georgia has a similar historical pattern. Beginning in 1831, Democratic governors led Georgia throughout the time of Jim Crow, Slave Codes, and segregation. Democrats have held the office of governor in Tennessee for many consecutive years. The vast majority of southern states all share the same legacy. Southern democrats attempted to keep blacks enslaved economically, socially, and educationally even when physical slavery was made illegal. This was accomplished by a calculated plan to infiltrate government and capitalize on the ignorance of newly freed blacks.

David Pilgrim, professor of sociology at Ferris State University is quoted as writing, "Many blacks resisted the indignities of Jim Crow, and, far too often, they paid for their bravery with their lives." This 2012 conclusion comes on the banner of the Jim Crow Museum of Racist Memorabilia at a university in Michigan. The museum houses a large collection of Mammy figurines, a cadre of "white only" and "colored" signs, as well as a life sized replica of a lynching tree and a quantitative display of the n* word. This collection is said to make visitors cringe. Curated by Pilgrim, a black man, the museum boasts a 1.3 million dollar gallery endowment. The Ferris State University archive is the largest public collection of racist memorabilia from segregation to reconstruction, the Civil Rights movement and beyond.

Pilgrim attests to the 'beyond' by including caricatures of President Obama eating a banana, and modern advertising of products like Aunt Jemima syrups and bleaching creams. These symbols' prevalence in our society extend the effects of the southern racist past by hiding behind the comedic side of stereotype in characters like Eddie Murphy's Buckwheat and Tyler Perry's Madea. Eventually these characters are ingratiated into African-American subculture by those they portray, normalizing segregation and annihilating assimilation.

The groundwork for these and other offences were nurtured and protected by the Democrat-dominated South. Jim Crow laws were an institutionalized construct whose sole purpose was to keep the descendants of slaves "in their place." This was the ultimate payback for the loss of the Civil War. It began with the passage of laws, post Reconstruction, regarding transportation. Years later, Dr. Martin Luther King, Jr. and other activists would use modes of travel to begin their counter protests in Montgomery, Alabama.

In this period of systematic racism in the south, the idea of favoring persons of mixed African heritage were abandoned for a more poignant approach meant to permanently delay the black man's striving for complete freedom. Segregation, much like the infiltration of the Nazi regime throughout Europe, spread to city parks, cemeteries, theaters, and restaurants which was eventually codified by state and local legislators throughout the south. Inferiority was the moniker for ethnic minorities remained prevalent throughout the 1960's despite the unconstitutionality of doctrines like Separate, But Equal.

While racial striving existed in the North, it was notably more cruel in the Democrat-dominated South which was evidenced not only by the plethora of overt and systematic racism, but also by the 1968 Democratic presidential candidate and former Governor of Alabama, George Wallace. Wallace, whose campaign centered around segregation and populism ran unsuccessfully four times in his bid for the presidency. However, the deep state of racism in the south was strongly expressed even in his defeat as the states of Alabama, Georgia, Louisiana, Mississippi, and Arkansas all remained Democrat. 90% of black voters in those states voted for Wallace even though he physically took a personal and public stance against integration by blocking the entrance to the University of Alabama. Wallace's campaign can only be explained by saying that blacks had been convinced that 'separate, but equal' was either (1) better for them, or (2) all they could ever hope for.

Wallace's campaign was symptomatic of the ideology common to the Democrat south.

His approval of the beating of Selma protest marchers was just one of many examples of the great lengths he would go through to keep blacks impoverished. After the Civil Rights movement, Wallace recanted his strong positions against integration; but his affiliation with the party lines that supported him, Democrats, were far from over.

Democrat control, however, has never been relegated solely to the south. Cities like Detroit, Baltimore, and Chicago have long been under 100% Democrat control yet the cities themselves are urban war-torn examples of the plight of post-slavery blacks. When you considered that blacks were not even allowed to attend the Democratic National Convention until 1924, [2] it is surprising that it was as early as the Truman administration that an all out political courting of the black American population began.

---

[2] https://www.factcheck.org/2008/04/blacks-and-the-democratic-party/

In 1948, Harry Truman received 77% of the African American vote in his presidential race. Truman, a Democrat, brought forth an Executive Order that prohibited racist bias in federal hiring practices, including military appointments. That singular act began a public effort to convert former black Republicans to the Democrat Party. Prior to this decree, black populations had few clear paths to attain middle class status in America, especially in the south. The military and other government jobs became the first of many great equalizers which provided exposure and opportunity for the descendants of former slaves. The opportunity to leave the proverbial plantation of the agrarian south was well overdue and forever altered the mindset of Democratic leadership. Truman's New Deal Coalition rallied special interest groups and voting blocs to support Democratic candidates through the early 1960's. The need for 'relief' jobs, especially unionized opportunities like garbage collectors, machine operators, assembly line workers, and the like, were at all-time highs. This new level of 'prosperity' shifted public opinion from the Republican party to the Democrat Party, especially for those seeking an immediately level of prosperity.

For the first time in a generation, blacks held a level of civility only experienced by white populations. However, community schools, hospitals, centers of higher education, and training facilities were still lacking in these communities. The new black middle class peaked and plateaued all in the same decade. Salaries were capped by large unions. Limits on promotion, regulation with regard to growth potential, and other glass ceilings kept blacks in the lower middle class strata for more than 100 years.

Like an natural survivor, most African Americans developed elaborate methods of creating communal networks within their communities which allowed them to revel in the new freedom they experienced, even though the standard of living was far below their Constitutional right to pursue.

This lock on votes, fortunately, was severely fractured in the north because the Civil Rights movement and the continual oppression of minorities led to the collapse of Truman's New Deal. Voter loyalties which had been tied to lower-middle class advances became exploited by social forces who were the culprits in the first place. Republicans fought to give blacks all of the Constitutional freedoms every citizen was given the right to enjoy. Democrats blocked access to those freedoms, especially in the south and instituted a cultural racism that crushed the spirits of the ethnic minority. Years later, under one Executive Order and one Act, the sitting President gave back portions of the freedoms they had been afforded by the Constitution hundreds of years prior.

The Bottom Line

- 'Separate, but equal' was a doctrine promoted by members of the Democrat party.

- The Democrat-led south maintained a system of legal oppression, disenfranchisement, and racial segregation created a gulf between whites and blacks in America.
- President Truman used an Executive Order to give blacks portions of freedoms the Constitution already guaranteed, which had not been enforced under Jim Crow.
- President Trump signed Executive Orders which lifted the black unemployment rate, relieved burdens on our criminal justice system through the First and Second Step Act, and re-ignited interest into Opportunity Zones which bring investment options to black communities.

JFK and the Democrats

Photo by History in HD on Unsplash

Characteristically different from any other president, John Fitzgerald "Jack" Kennedy was the embodiment of a knight in shining armour. His widow, Jacqueline, was quoted as saying, when referring to the charm and charisma that characterized her husband and his presidency, "Don't let it be forgot, that once there was a spot, for one brief, shining moment that was known as Camelot. There'll be great presidents again … but there will never be another Camelot."

"The Rights of Man" was, one source claims, the original platform for the Democrat Party. To that same motto, and in times of national trials, the urge to secure rights of the individual, even over the collective nation, became foremost. In 1960, this was the mantra by which the party would promote John Fitzgerald Kennedy as the nominee.

Republicans had lost pre-eminence seven years before. The Soviets were leading the space race. Chinese and Russian satellites filled the atmosphere. Conservative tendencies to strengthen US military was one of the initial focal points of the Democrat Party that eventually fell by the wayside. Communist pressures in Western

Europe drew alliances between other first world nations in order to suppress the Soviet Union and other nations in opposition to capitalism; and a United States' commitment to the United Nations charter was intended to resist aggression in the East. The non-communist nations in Asia, Africa, and Latin America were charged with creating working partnerships based on a respect that there is no room for second class citizens in the modern world. This was the premise behind JFK's plan of integration for America.

Blacks and whites both struggled from holes in the Taft-Hartley Act and the Wagner Acts which were designed to protect the right to work. The right to a job requires action to break down artificial and arbitrary barriers to employment based on age, race, sex, religion, or national origin originated during this season in American politics.

Unemployment strikes hardest at workers over 40, minority groups, young people, and women. We will not achieve full employment until prejudice against these workers is wiped out, according to stats taken from the time.

When elected, Kennedy was the youngest President elected as well as the first and only Roman Catholic to date. While in the Senate he won a Pulitzer for his book Profiles in Courage. Kennedy was also the first President to have served in the Navy. This made him an attractive choice for both Democrats and Republican-voting citizens who were frustrated by domestic and international tensions. Even though Kennedy was brought under fire for his youth and religion, his appeal to multiple generations was made evident when the first televised Presidential debates gave him the edge over Nixon.

While Kennedy only served as President for two years, from 1961–1963, his Administration was fraught with controversy. That controversy over segregation, America's involvement in the Vietnam conflict, and the raising head of communism kept Kennedy on the edge of public opinion, ultimately ending in his death from assassination.

Before that fatal shot rang out from the grassy knoll in Dallas, Kennedy launched a campaign that was supported by Democratic leaders Lyndon Johnson, Adlai Stevenson, and Hubert Humphrey. However, after his victory, his stance on integration and desire to stay out of international conflict made him a target within his own party.

Kennedy in Dallas, November 1963

Democrats found in President Kennedy criticism at every turn. Whether it was his lack of experience, ultra-religious stance, anti-labor loyalty, or the disdain of party leaders, Kennedy often found himself at odds with many Democrats. His campaign appealed to black voters making his administration one that had to be dealt with in a much different manner than others as Democrats had come to rely heavily on black voters to remain in power. President Kennedy's assassination was one that caused a great controversy in how Americans viewed politicians and terrorists. It was the first of several acts of domestic terrorist acts against our sovereignty in the last century but has since been forgotten, by most, as a stain on our way of governing.

Yet Kennedy's assassination brought to the forefront of public discussion the notion that those in politics do not always serve the interest of the people. With regard to his election and his mere two years in office, the overall establishment presumption was one of disgust for the man in the Oval Office who wanted to avoid war. Warmongers in the United States understood the invariable influx of money to be made if the nation continued or escalated the war effort with the communists. Kennedy had made campaign pledges to stay out of Vietnam regardless of the aftermath. Most of his presidency was consumed with talks about going to war against the Soviet Union installations discovered in Cuba. With the potential for a global thermonuclear conflict looming, Kennedy used diplomacy to stay off an invasion. Many in Washington rejected the idea of diplomacy with the communists and insisted on escalating the conflicts, especially Kennedy's successor, President Lyndon B. Johnson.

Johnson was more of a status quo Democrat of this era. He took marines into a full scale conflict in Vietnam in 1965, and is quotes by the University of Virginia[3] as saying,

---

[3] https://prde.upress.virginia.edu/content/Vietnam

"I guess we've got no choice, but it scares the death out of me. I think everybody's going to think, 'we're landing the Marines, we're off to battle.'"

Johnson, dispatched 3,500 soldiers to South Vietnam for part of a three year program of sustained bombing in North Vietnam. While some historians would rationalize Johnson's acts as characteristic of those 'inherited' and 'inevitable' decisions left by the Kennedy assassination, Johnson's vow not to lose the war was the driving force behind the lengthy campaign he launched into the generations-long conflict between the Viet Cong army (South Vietnamese and Cambodian) and the communist in North Vietnam. While Kennedy had been a war hero by serving in the Second World War, Johnson, who was only in active military for one year,[4] was more along the lines of a career politician.

4

https://en.wikipedia.org/wiki/Salamaua%E2%80%93Lae_campaign

The cold war still scratching at the door of the White House even after the Vietnam conflict came to an end thanks to American contributions in 1973 (battles officially ended in 1975) with a signing of the Paris Peace Accords, Cuba now became the top priority. By this time Richard Nixon was in office and JFK's strategies regarding the nation might be revitalized through Nixon. Having been Vice President under Eisenhower, when the Bay of Pigs battle was first initiated, Nixon understood and planned to capitalize on ending communism in our hemisphere through an invasion of Cuba. Like Kennedy, however, Nixon's presidency was cut short - not because of assassination, but resignation due to scandal.

Johnson's escalation in Vietnam resulted in Americans having to contend with the largest influx (still over 7 million cases in 2013, 3 million of which were active duty) of veteran PTSD (15.2%) and other traumatic cases which overran the Veterans

Administration (VA) budget, plunging our nation into domestic debt. Vietnam is considered a "pharmacological" war in which soldiers were exposed to various chemical combatants, a treatment for which was not readily available. The costs for this war continue to be $22 billion dollars **per year**, in payables to the veterans and their families. The Vietnam War conflict continues to make up just under 6% of our national debt these almost 50 years later. That is a total outlay of $572 billion dollars in treatment alone. An additional $141 billion was spent over fourteen years on comparative reparations in Vietnam[5] and the cost of the lives of 56,000 service men and women.

Economists give further credit for global inflationary repercussions for the conflict in Vietnam. Johnson is criticized for implementing a 'Great Society' domestic plan while funding global conflicts without

---

[5] https://www.nytimes.com/1975/05/01/archives/us-spent-141billion-in-vietnam-in-14-years.html

securing increased federal funds. This was the cause for the decline in United States purchasing power worldwide. In short, Democrat policies weakened the national budget to such a degree Americans are still paying the price for decisions that penalize African Americans more than any other ethnic group.

The Bottom Line

- Global tensions, conflicts, and competitions were the perfect distraction from mounting domestic problems in America.
- The assassination of President Kennedy introduced a period of domestic upheaval as the nation continued to struggle to end the legal racism and discrimination against African Americans.
- President Johnson's Great Society dramatically worked against black economic power as it failed to provide services needed by black communities to overcome Jim Crow.

- Democrats in the presidency committed American to a multi-billion annual bill for the Vietnam war that we are still paying in benefits and reparations.

Neo Liberalism

Many folks might say that the 'liberal' period of the Democrat party ended in 1968, after the Kennedy and Johnson era ended. The center-left leadership of Carter, Clinton, and Obama resembled, to some, a return to the New Deal or Great Society. For blacks today, 84% of whom lean or affiliate Democrat according to Pew research (2017), the idea of being center-left has changed from the Kennedy era. Arguably, the center line has shifted creating an opportunity for neo liberalism in the Left's camp which only appears to be more centrist. In fact, many could argue that our entire political spectrum has shifted creating more of a bell shaped curve than a traditional spectrum with opposing views minimizing at either end. The center progression shows the shifting in how "centrist" views have changed over the decades.

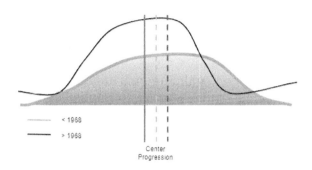

Seventy years ago, LGBTQ tendencies were viewed as abnormal, deviant, and even criminal. The first state to decriminalize same-sex intercourse was Illinois in 1962. But it would take nearly a decade for the second state to jump on board. Sixteen states, Puerto Rico, and parts of Missouri still had anti-LBGTQ laws on the books in the 2000's. Our nation went from one extreme, Thomas Jefferson proposed castration for any male participating in sodomy, to an open acceptance and re-definition of traditional marriage in all 50 states. Long before legislation caught up, laws banning 'alternative' lifestyles stopped being enforced in most major cities decades prior. However, the shift in normalizing homosexual and other lifestyles saw a steady progression of changing views both on main street and at the polls.

The path to legalizing marijuana use has followed a similar pattern in the legislature. A weakening American consciousness regarding social drug use, especially depressants such as alcohol or cannabis, combined with the strong advocacy originating out of California kept the conversation open regarding legalization of the substance. A twenty year battle by the National Organization for the Reform of Marijuana Laws to downgrade marijuana from a Class 1 drug failed in the 1990's. [6] Nevertheless, the lack of violence associated with cannabis use resulted in a level of tolerance and recreational use

---

[6] https://www.ibtimes.com/why-marijuana-schedule-i-drug-1821426

spread with the post-Berkeley culture which saw broadening use by Caucasian youth. Where earlier generations saw cannabis use as a primarily black and Hispanic drug, racial links toward keeping the drug Class 1 were highlighted in 1974 by a southern Senator who testified before the Senate subcommittee saying, "If the cannabis epidemic continues to spread at the rate of the post-Berkeley period, we may find ourselves saddled with a large population of semi-zombies – of young people acutely afflicted by the amotivational syndrome."

James Oliver Eastland, D-Miss, the "Voice of the White South," became known as the Godfather of Mississippi politics and strongly advocated against (racial) integration. Part of the resistance, he was quoted as referencing blacks as inferior- as a group of people plagued with this 'amotivational syndrome.' An attorney, cotton plantation owner, and State Senator, Eastland was appointed by Governor Paul Johnson, Sr. to fill the open position left by Pat Harrison's death. It may be largely presumed that Eastland's radical racism contributed to the long-fettered fight to declassify marijuana for the fear he successfully communicated to the subcommittee. When rising to the rank of President pro tempore of the Senate and Chairman of the Senate Judiciary Committee in the 1970's, his influence expanded. Eastland resigned in light of Nixon's Watergate Impeachment hearings, weeks before the end of his final term.

Despite Eastland's prejudice toward marijuana, its widespread use became folly to mainstream America. Hippie culture spread through music, college communities, and the failed support for the Vietnam conflict, especially among young people. Seen as a harmless but wasted community, recreational users were scoffed but tolerated. Still assimilation of hippie culture remained mainstream, and with it, recreational marijuana use.

Ultimately, ideologies characterized as alternative due to the nature of their recreational expression became exploited by the liberal political movement. The perceived failure of traditional values solidified by the collapse of the family began to reveal itself among lower socio-economic groups as early as the 1980's. President Lyndon Johnson's War on Poverty legislation (the Economic Opportunity Act) was ultimately rejected by Nixon's administration. Yet neither president delivered on reducing the 17% poverty rate below 10% until now. To paint a more complete portrait it is important to note that among certain groups, the poverty rate far exceeded the national rate significantly.

From 1965 until recent years, the poverty rate amongst senior citizens was nearly 30%. Virtually one in three seniors were impoverished. While some of LBJ's social programs initially counteracted the decline in poverty which began in the 1950's, poverty among those under 18 years of age remained at 20% even in the Obama era. 12.1 million children were living in poverty in 2004, and nearly 12% of Americans overall. Numbers among ethnically diverse, immigrant, and other typically marginalized populations exceeded national standards in a similar way. Essentially, before President Trump's administration, 1 in 4 children in America were impoverished.

Some economists, including Milton Friedman, have argued that Johnson's policies actually had a negative impact on the economy because of their interventionist nature, noting in a PBS interview that "the government sets out to elimi-nate poverty, it has a war on poverty,

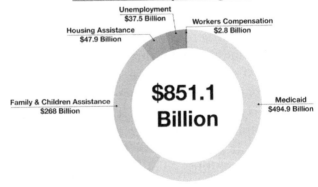

so-called "poverty" increases. It has a welfare program, and the welfare program leads to an expansion of problems. A general attitude develops that government isn't a very efficient way of doing things."[7] Those adhering to a similar ideology chiefly recommend that the best way to fight poverty is not through government spending but through widespread economic growth.[8] The later is precisely what President Trump implemented from day one of taking office in 2016.

---

[7] Friedman, Milton (August 9, 2002). "First Measured Century: Interview: Milton Friedman". PBS. Archived from the original on August 8, 2002. Retrieved May 21, 2013.

[8] Priest, George L. (April 11, 2013). "Poverty, Inequality and Economic Growth: Simple Principles" (PDF). Yale University. Retrieved May 21, 2013.

Baetjer Jr., Howard (April 2003). "Does Welfare Diminish Poverty?". *Foundation for Economic Freedom*. Retrieved May 21, 2013.

Loo, Dennis (April 2003). "Libertarianism and Poverty". *The Ethical Spectacle*. Retrieved May 21, 2013.

Neither Friedman, nor criticisms of President Johnson's plan by Dr. Martin Luther King kept the "War on Poverty" from continuing spending from the Office of Economic Opportunity until recent years. America taxpayers have averaged $15 trillion in funding allocated to programs like medicaid, medicare, food stamps, and job core according to the Cato Institute, a liberal think tank. Despite those expenditures the rate of poverty remained the same as it was during Johnson's administration; even in the face of President Clinton's initiatives to revise and revitalize the battle against poverty in the 1980-1990's with the Personal Responsibility and Work Opportunity Act in which he "ended (traditional) welfare."

Criticisms, especially among middle class white Americans, were in strong opposition to the welfare state being promoted by political liberals. A change in strategy was strongly needed if funding for these social programs would remain part of big government, notably since poverty continued to rise in spite of the growing budget expenditures to alleviate said poverty. Enter the new liberal agenda based in the racist ideology of Ford's Great Society. Nixon-led scandals, appointments, and regret of America at war gave way to the nomination of Gerald Ford, a modest Republican with a long tenure as a US Representative. Ford, considering himself more of a diplomatic leader, made several crucial decisions while in office that gave a blind reprieve to liberals planning their twenty-year coup of American politics.

First, the pardon of former President Nixon in 1974.

Secondly, a conditional amnesty to Vietnam draft dodgers in that same year (full pardons came under President Carter).

Finally, and most impacting was Ford's response to the growing inflation crisis in the nation and ethnic warring in Asia.

Again relying on diplomacy, Ford, a Republican ubiquitously dubbed President NiceGuy, passed responsibility to answer the abortion question on to the states but later recanted his neutrality when outed by his wife, an iconic feminist, on a 60 Minutes interview. Later he came out as Pro Choice. Halting aid to Israel in response to the Arab-Israeli conflict rounded out some of the negative policies enacted under President Ford. Although none could argue that after a period of international skirmishes and President Nixon's near impeachment America needed time to heal. Ford, however, took measures that would only years later reveal the cost of American passivity in domestic and foreign policies that contributed to the global loss of life (in Asia), systematic decline of the American family values (through domestic positions on abortion, sexual orientation, the ERA, and drugs), and the beginning of failed negotiations in the middle east.

In this period of neoliberalism, political branding shifted. Republicans had much saving face to devote their time to -

rebuilding the diplomatic administration under Ford to resemble something a bit more rugged wasn't easy. The nasty little things Americans, especially conservative Americans, had been reluctant to speak about were making their way to the nightly news. Things like drug abuse, urban crime, school failures, incurable disease, alternative sexual lifestyles, and America's failures abroad were topics we'd hoped would fade into the background. Instead racial tensions continued at home in the 1970's and the other things folded themselves into the American fabric like a well worn patch. In order to maintain power, mastermind marketers took to task and began creating what we now see as the Democrat party.

Ford had been appointed and won the nomination against Ronald Reagan. Reagan, a "Republican's Republican" would become a larger figure years later. The 1976 Republican National Convention was held in the Kansas City, Missouri. Within just more than 100 votes, actor and future conservative poster boy Ronald Reagan lost his party's nod in favor of President NiceGuy, Gerald Ford, an establishment-man. Betty Ford's reputation superseded her husband's and their campaign of transparency didn't resonate with enough voters to outright win the presidency but it did get him enough votes to face the Democratic challenger. One journalists writes of Reagan's speech after failing to gain the party nomination:

Would they say, "Thank God for those people in 1976 who headed off that loss of freedom; who kept us now a hundred years later free; who kept our world from nuclear destruction?" This was this generation's challenge, Reagan declared. "Whether [the Americans of 2076] have the freedom that we have known up until now will depend on what we do here."

The man they called too old and too conservative to lead the country would have to wait another four years to reap the rewards of victory and epitomize Gorbachev's defeat.

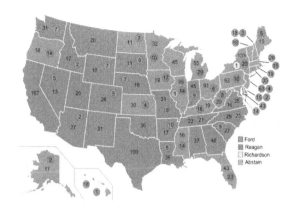

Credit: Ariostos - Own work, CC BY-SA 3.0

President James Earl "Jimmy" Carter, Jr. took office in 1977 with Walter Mondale as his Vice President. After the first 100 days, Carter backed down on his domestic and foreign policy including SALT (Strategic Arms Limitation Talks), peace talks in the middle east, and his battles with Congress over water construction projects, farm price subsidies, rebate proposals, education, national health care, and energy. He, Carter, was not one to support American Exceptionalism, and being from a rural upbringing, brought a new air of humility to the White House. His presidency, however, cannot be looked at as an ultimate failure when it comes to the middle east. Additionally, Carter played an important negative role at home in reference to the growing tensions with African Americans.

In his memoir, Carter fondly described growing up in rural Georgia alongside blacks who worked as field laborers in the peanut farming town of Plains. Despite "working alongside" blacks on the farm, Carter apparently failed to realize a need to adequately address the needs of urban populations who were being decimated by the remnants of systematic racism, drugs, and a growing subculture of violence. As part of the Democrat Party platform, Carter pushed for a form of nationalized health care. An outsider by any definition, Carter was also able to capitalize on the scandals that plagued both the previous Democratic and Republican administrations. His presidency was such a startling change from the standard political ambitions of his predecessors, he is still looked on favorably even though the hindsight view of the reputation he garnered as a diplomat in his 80's gave him more support than he ever earned while in office.

President Carter's bailout of the Chrysler corporation ($10.64 billion in 2018 dollars) and the fact that the nation would spend 444 days mourning the lives of Americans being held in the Iran hostage crisis were sad times for the Georgia native. Carter created a position for the now heavily criticized Department of Education and the Department of Energy, effectively expanding government in a very Democratic style. For as much as Carter intended to rid the global community of halted negotiations toward peace, his diplomatic failure to address the underlying relationship between the energy crisis and the extended unrest in the middle east followed up by an unprecedented corporate bailout in an industry contributing to the crisis led to an economic fallout at home.

The people most immediately affected by the economic recessions of the 1970's were inner city African Americans. Carter's pragmatism as a process-driven activist left much to be desired in the way of actual policy. You cannot, as president, spend your entire term in office discussing problems and not solving any. Stephen Hess, Senior Fellow Emeritus at Brookings used the acronym BOGSAT [Bunch of guys sitting around a table] to describe the end result of leadership like Carter's. [9] Welfare and tax reforms vacillated between processes in favor of centralization and decentralization without rhyme or any predictable pattern.

For some Americans of African descent, the 1970's were a decade of grandiose success across the country. Athletes like Arthur Ashe, Henry "Hank" Aaron, Wilt Chamberlain, Leroy "Satchel" Paige, Muhammad Ali, and Frank Robinson all had record breaking claims in the post Civil Rights decade. Politically an era of the"first black" person to do this and that began to

---

[9] https://www.brookings.edu/opinions/jimmy-carter-why-he-failed/

spring up well into Carter's tenure. Names like Andrew Young, Coleman Young, Shirley Chisholm, Kenneth Gibson, Thomas Bradley, Barbara Jordan, and Maynard Jackson, Jr. reached national acclaim for their respective races. Carter named the first African-American woman to the Cabinet by appointing her to run Housing and Urban Development (HUD).

Essence magazine was first published;

Roots first airs on prime time television;

the Supreme Court upheld affirmative action as a legal strategy; and

The Sugar Hill Gang released the first rap album Rapper's Delight.

There was unprecedented positive exposure for the black community in many ways. However, the average African American did not reap the direct rewards of these gains - no transactional exchange that made the day to day lives of average Americans of color improve. Contemporary literature told the story of urban families coping with the freedom of a post Jim Crow America and the tangible reality of latent racism in books and plays like The Bluest Eye (Toni Morrison, 1970), Maya Angelou's I Know Why the Caged Bird Sings (1970), and The River Niger (Joseph A. Walker, 1972), and in television with The Jefferson's and All in the Family.

After a decade in which civic leaders were murdered for enforcing the constitutional rights of African Americans, blacks found pride in the cultural pan-African movement which continued to draw people toward the Democrat Party. Yet, the day to day economic struggles of blacks, especially in urban areas, characterized the result of institutionalized racism that was reflective of the American south and other areas.

Rev. Dr. Martin Luther King, Jr. , an Independent, was murdered by a Democratic and communist sympathizer, James Earl Ray.

Malcolm X was murdered by Democrat and communist sympathizers, [member of] the Nation of Islam.

Medgar Evers was murdered by the White Citizens Council, an organization founded by Democrats.

The Mississippi Burning Murders were carried out by eight Klansman, an organization founded by and largely furthered by the Democrat Party.

In short, the day-to-day terror and economic thwarting of African Americans could be contributed to the Democrat Party's institutionalized entities that countered the directives given not only in the Constitution but also in its Amendments and Acts through subversive methodologies. However, Dr. King may have said it best when he was quoted in 1958:

> "Actually, the Negro has been betrayed by both the Republican and the Democrat Party. The Democrats have betrayed him by capitulating to the whims and caprices of the Southern Dixiecrats. The Republicans have betrayed him by capitulating to the blatant hypocrisy of reactionary right wing northern Republicans. And this coalition of southern Dixiecrats and right wing reactionary northern

Republicans defeats every bill and every move towards liberal legislation in the area of civil rights."

The Bottom Line

- The Democrat Party was the dominant political force behind the Ku Klux Klan.
- The need for the 14th Amendment to the Constitution was only an attempt to quell racial tensions in the south, not a failure in the Constitution itself.
- Political branding (advertising) shifted in the 1970's due largely to Republican silence and a period of black self-expression in activism, sports, and the arts.
- Liberal legislation in the way of Civil Rights is completely absent of any theory regarding liberalism today.

Black Power

The political slogan of the same name first gained prominence in the late 1960's and throughout the 1970's as an ideology aimed at achieving self-determination. While most of us have seen the single firsted salute and are well versed with the meaning of 'Black Power,' we may not have tied its origin back to recent history.

Let's face it, when the Black Power movement originated it was all about a return to Africa or afrocentricity. Yes, people marched in protest of what was happening at the time of the Civil Rights movement, but in all many wanted to return to the deeper roots blacks longed to discover.

The political and social goals were meant to overcome the social injustices and societal factors imposed post-reconstruction. Racial oppression, lack of established institutions that cater to the needs of blacks, and inadequate cooperatives, media, and small businesses which build strong local economies were absent. These and other objectives were part of a movement organized by Stokely Carmichael, Dr. Martin Luther King, Jr., other politicians and Richard Wright, an author of a 1954 book by the same nomenclature.

Photo Credit History in HD on Unsplash

Carmichael, and his co-organizer Willie Ricks, began the Student Nonviolent Coordinating Committee (SNCC) at Howard University. They saw "Black Power" as a means of black solidarity and wanted more than Rev. King's desegregation movement seemed to offer. Unlike Reverend King's nonviolent protests demanding "Freedom Now" SNCC organizers wanted to form political affiliations in which blacks would elect leaders that could better represent them. Discussions between black nationalists, along the lines of Carmichael and Rev. King, were conversely represented by ideals of black separatism of groups like the Black Panthers, led by Bobby Seale, and other offshoot efforts under the umbrella of African Internationalism or pan-Africanism, as well as the NAACP (National Association for the Advancement of Colored People) and the Nation of Islam.

From the mid 1960's on, afrocentric hairstyles and clothing infiltrated communities across the nation, especially among young people. Protests like the the one pictured here were commonplace. But the manifest destiny blacks should have had as a result was achieved from a radical left flank, according to sociologist Herbert Haines. Not from the peaceful protests led by historic figures like Dr. King. Haines studied the correlation between the Civil Rights Movement and the Black Power movement at the State University of New York. Haines contends that the impact of radical or militant Black Power groups created a 'crisis in American institutions' that demanded that black issues be on the forefront of the national political agenda.

This 'crisis' couldn't have been more thoroughly depicted than by the 1968 Summer Olympics' award ceremony for the 200 meter sprint held in Mexico City. Americans Tommie Smith and John Carlos won their event (pictured) and forever illustrated the struggle for black excellence in a single moment with clenched fists raised in the air. Smith, who was 24 years old at the time, broke the 20 second barrier (legally) for the first time when he won gold. He and teammate Carlos stood atop the podium wearing a black gloved hand, black socks, and held one shoe in their hands. This symbolism remains a defining moment in the Black Power movement and brought worldwide attention to a national problem. The athletes bare feet were meant to represent African-American poverty back home. Australian athlete Peter Norman, who shared the podium with them as the silver medalist, participated in the silent protest by wearing a OPHR (Olympic Project for Human Rights) badge. Ultimately, Smith and Carlos were suspended from the games by IOC President, Avery Brundage, a man they protested prior to competition.

Photo Credit Angelo Cozzi, public domain Getty Images

By March 1972, the Black Power movement became more organized, resulting in the formation of the National Black Political Convention held in Gary, Indiana. Although criticized by NAACP leadership, the convention had specific goals relating to congressional elections, control of community schools, and national health insurance. The resulting outcomes did not directly impact immediate policy but rather began the dialogue of, "the nature of American society and the place of the African American in it."

Whether merely targeting encouragement for participation or advanced quota systems, Affirmative Action was an effective outcome of the Black Power movement. Affirmative Action in America which was initially used to combat racial discrepancies in hiring practices was first created during the Kennedy Administration by Executive Order in 1961. It was later signed into law by Lyndon Johnson in 1965, and included provisions against gender discrimination as well. Executive Order 11246 replaced the original action and re-affirmed the government's commitment to end employment discrimination. The Act was also meant to put pressure on institutions to abide by the 1964 Voting Rights Act. As recent as 2003, however, courts in Washington, California, and Michigan have ruled that institutions of higher learning may not use Affirmative Action as a means of admitting students. Cases such as these continue to challenge whether or not Affirmative Action is applicable in society today and to what extent legislation is needed to protect individuals based on race, ethnicity, creed, gender, color, or national origin.

Of course, the pinnacle of the Black Power is not Affirmative Action anyway. It was the awareness of the need for self-determination, a need that some would say is still lost on people of color. The number of blacks who currently rely on government social services to make ends meet has risen over the years. According to online journalists, more than 1 in 3 Americans receive some level of public assistance in 2014. 35% of Americans, 100 million people receive food stamps through the Supplemental Nutrition Assistance Program (15%), Medicaid (26%), or welfare (26%).[10] Of those states whose residents are on the receiving end, California and the District of Columbia top the list. On average, nearly half of all recipients remain on public assistance for 3-4 years. During that time, families spend approximately 77% of their income on basic necessities including housing, transportation, and food; which compares to the 65% most families not receiving assistance spend. However, when you consider that financial planners recommend that housing account for only 25-33% of your monthly income, and transportation spending averaging around 10-15% we can see that even families who are ineligible for public assistance still spend too high a percentage on basic needs.

It is difficult to determine why this trend of high spending on basic needs is found in

---

[10] https://www.creditdonkey.com/welfare-statistics.html

lower socioeconomic families, however, it is likely that higher interest rates, lower equity, and lack of wealth planning knowledge greatly contribute. Furthermore, the inevitable emergency that can affect wealth stability are more likely to debilitate families on the lower end of the wealth spectrum simply because the financial safety net is smaller to begin with.

Financial strategists advise families to develop nest eggs with 3-6 months of operating expenses within them. This means saving enough money to cover all of your expenses for that length of time - in its entirety. Include gas, food, utilities, and of course, the big things like mortgage, rent, and car payments in these calculations. These strategists do not give the option to choose the expenses you save for - their recommendation is the same no matter what your monthly debt is, or the limitations on your income. Most lower to middle class families only have 3-6 weeks worth of savings. While impoverished families may only have 3-6 days worth of savings, if that. In short, families are either preparing to go into a financial crisis, are currently in a financial crisis, or have just come out of one. The ability to have a financial nest egg keeps some families afloat while others are derailed for months or more. That is the essence of what Black Power sought to inspire black families to overcome- the continual sinking that occurs when financial crises arise. We will all go through one or more, every ten years, experts say. But for black families that were economically compromised by Democrat-dominated leadership, bad luck, poor planning, racism, or ignorance, coming back from those crises have been nearly impossible for decades. It was for this cause that the Black Power movement made such an impact on people in America, and worldwide. Black Power movements sprung up in other countries where large black populations were found such as in Brazil and Jamaica. Even Black Lives Matter is a kind of Black Power movement.

However, when black people began investing in their own communities and taking pride in their ethnicity, in being black, Democrats devised another way to compromise the community. Legalized abortion might have begun with a white woman, but it was black women that ultimately became the target of the Pro Choice movement through an organization called Planned Parenthood.

Regardless of the perception of Planned Parenthood as an organization, it is important to simply look at the facts behind its attack on people of color.

1. According to the CDC (Centers for Disease Control), a black child is twice as likely to be killed in the womb than a white child.
2. 1 out of every 4 abortions is carried out at a Planned Parenthood facility.
3. Even though Planned Parenthood reported $85 million in profits in 2008, they still applied for and received nearly $350 million in government grants.
4. According to the American Life League's 2011 report, greater than 97% of Planned Parenthood services are abortions. Less than 3% of their services nationally are for "health

care," and this includes adoption referrals in the totals. In other words, abortion is Planned Parenthood's primary business.

5. Margaret Sanger, the founder of the organization that became Planned Parenthood, was a racist who was regularly quoted as saying, "We do not want the word to go out that we want to exterminate the Negro population and the minister is the man who can straighten that idea out if it ever occurs to any of their more rebellious members," in her writings called The Negro Project.

6. Planned Parenthood provides "comprehensive sex education" in America's high schools but over 3.2 million teenaged girls have sexually transmitted diseases. Planned Parenthood is NOT effective in reducing the cases of STDs.

7. Planned Parenthood has been carrying out a plan of genocide in the black community for over 103 years, keeping our birthing numbers low and thereby diminishing out vote.

8. In states with predominantly white populations, states like North Dakota, Idaho, Kentucky, Rhode Island, South Dakota, West Virginia, and Hawaii, to name a few, there are 3 or fewer Planned Parenthood facilities in the entire state. North Dakota, for example, has zero facilities and South Dakota only has one. 78% of Planned Parenthood's clinics are in minority communities. [When I was growing up in Atlanta, there were two Planned Parenthood clinics within walking distance to the poor neighborhood where I lived, but, there were zero full service grocery stores, zero gas stations, and zero parks within that same radius.]
9. The Democrat Party has officially been the Pro Choice party ever since abortion was made legal in 1973 even though it is mostly black families that are affected by abortion. In the late 1970's, the Republican Party took a firm stand for life, drawing more pro choice voters to the Democrat Party.
10. Planned Parenthood and the Democrat Party have joined forces to legislate

and advocate for Pro Choice rhetoric as a healthcare issue, not an abortion issue.

Through their systematic and malicious undoing of the Black Power movement through abortion, Planned Parenthood and the Democrat Party have effectively eliminated 15.5 million African Americans since 1973, according to the US Center for Disease Control National Vital Statistics Reports (see graph below). That is more than deaths contributed to heart disease, AIDS, accidents, violent crime, and cancer combined. African Americans are disproportionately affected by abortion, not because the choice to abortion is an ethnic tradition. This could not be farther from the truth. When the Black Power movement encouraged African Americans to demand their full rights under the US Constitution, a strong push, called the Negro Plan, went into a more strategic phase by partnering with abortion providers across the nation. The Democrat Party, who receives annual donations from Planned Parenthood, took us the Pro Choice cause as a way of controlling black populations with targeting advertising that promotes abortion as the only option for an unplanned pregnancy. Furthermore, Democrat-dominated cities have kept blacks from having self-sufficiency centered wrap-around services, and access to clear pathways to economic opportunity; thereby making the option of abortion more attractive to couples experiencing an unplanned pregnancy.

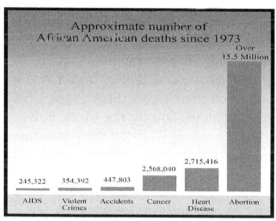

Photo Credit
http://www.blackgenocide.org/black.html

According to BlackGenocide.org, black women only make up about 13% of the child-bearing population in America. Yet, they are the victims of 36% of all abortions in the nation. "According to the Alan Guttmacher Institute, black women are more than 5 times as likely as white women to have an abortion. On average, 1,876 black babies are aborted every day in the United States," states the organization. Historically speaking, "choice" has been a word associated with genocide, the extermination of an ethnic group. It is fitting that as soon as blacks began rising up to demand their rights through the Civil Rights movement, and by the Black Power movement, a stronger, more sinister effort was made legal by the Supreme Court. A comparison of language used in both the Holocaust and in slavery show the pattern followed by eugenists who want to see a permanent end to black power.

"Parasites" and "bacilli" were words used by Nazis to describe Jews and others targeted for extermination.

Benjamin Rush, a leading American scientist who personally opposed slavery, speculated that all blacks were really leprous, diseased, whites in need of a cure.

In his medical textbook Abortion Practice, Warren Hern analogizes the unwanted, unborn child to a disease, the treatment of choice for which is abortion.

In each case, the person who was to be exterminated was compared to a disease, vermin, or other lower life forms whose life opponents were justified to take. This is how many early Democrats saw African Americans. Margaret Sanger, and others like her, have slowly manipulated ministers, doctors, and the Civil Rights movement itself to promote abortion on demand to black women. The 2009 documentary Maafa 21 was created to document black genocide from slavery to abortion, using some of the same arguments, some say, as the Black Panthers and the Nation of Islam.

The Bottom Line

1. The Black Power movement came in many forms but was collectively aimed at rebuilding the African American community after slavery.
2. Black Power began in the 1960's but still lasts today from groups like Black Lives Matter.
3. Planned Parenthood began a campaign targeting African Americans during the Black Power Movement.
4. Planned Parenthood is the greatest killer of African Americans in the world, through abortion.
5. Black power and black genocide are still in a struggle against one another.
6. The Democrat Party is a supporter of black genocide through economic impoverishment, abortion, and corruption in the criminal justice system in predominantly black communities.

Government Cheese

Did you not pour me out like milk and curdle me like cheese?
~ Job 10: 10

Photo Credit Bettmann Archive/Getty Images

Without resorting to statistic, let us lean an ear toward a personal story of Democrat-controlled communities and the plight of those individuals whose families lived under the thumb of ethnic control policies that America once embraced. The Economic Policy Institute revisited the federal role in the creation of government housing projects in 2012. Their conclusions support the personal narratives that follow.

As far as the eye could travel was the depths at which black faces emerged from behind brick walled buildings that had been constructed originally for poor whites. These housing 'projects' or ghettos as they were frequently called, were built to last. The one my family lived in was built prior to my mother's birth and was equipped to last her entire life. These apartment styled structures had no air conditioning, no modern conveniences like washer and dryer connections, nor dishwashers. There was a clothesline installed in the small patch of back yard collectively shared between the inhabitants of a particular building. In the Grady Homes project where I resided for much of my formative years there was a familial association amongst us children. Of the senior citizens the same was true. The parents and other adults, conversely, did not always accept the same building-family assimilation thereby limiting the amount of community-building that could take place in this small urban oasis.

Violence, of course, was the soundtrack looping through our lives - the sirens, the yelling, the slamming of doors, the sounds of silence when the electricity was turned off, the roar of the public transit that echoed around the perimeter of our world. On one hand, there was a grocery store and a convenience store in walking distance. I remember my grandmother planning our nearly daily trips to the market at the end of our street, on the 'curb.' When funds, even public funds gained through social services were not available, we walked to the Candy Lady's apartment to buy an egg- not a dozen eggs mind you, or a cup of milk, or a piece of candy for pennies on the dollar. This is the commerce of the ghetto.

Every other week during the season the Watermelon Man rode through in his Ford pick up, loaded full of watermelons or other produce. A handful of, often shirtless, teen aged boys straddled the back of the truck bed or rode shotgun, hoping out at every stop to service the local customer base. The Lays potato chip man also came by, more frequently, and handed out the stale remnants of the vending machines he maintained from one of the high rise office buildings that made up the backdrop of our community portrait. We could see the wealth of our city at a near distance but we were logistically miles away from acquiring an inch of the American dream of wealth.

Back then, schools were the center of our community; not the church, and not anything else. The school was the invisible gateway to ending ghetto life in America, or so they told us. It was there, back when teachers were respected and homework expected. Then that our parents and grandparents placed the importance on the next generation, those of us who never experienced Jim Crow first hand. Of course the church was there. The imposing edifice lorded over the skyline of typical urban centers. Their steeples towering over, interrupting the landscape with their stained glass and closed doors. Nearly if not every Sunday afternoon you could spot the church van dropping off little children who were dressed in their best. These 'Sunday-orphans' ran home to Momma, and were rarely greeted by Daddy. But parents weren't legally obligated to send their children to church. Hence, school became the center of ghetto life for children.

This generation, of which I am a part, embodied the hopes of the previous one; a generation who remembered segregation. A generation who resented and distrusted, in many cases, white people, especially white men. Our parents endured entering through back doors, survived the dilapidation of separate but equal, and recognized the need to pour back into the minds of the young people in our community. While that notion has not faded from the consciousness of the black community today, one thing had changed. Drugs, jail, and the grave have impacted the community to such a degree that mothers do not train their children the way past generations did. They do not reinforce the expectation nor the importance of education. This is not for neglect, but a priority to deal with the pressures of economic enslavement and frustrated futures. They have bowed down to the victimhood propaganda and have taken comfort in it.

> A claim by U.S. Secretary of Education Arne Duncan, referring to former New York City Schools Chancellor Joel Klein, is one. Mr. Duncan said: "Klein knows, as I do, that great teachers can transform a child's life chances—and that poverty is not destiny. It's a belief deeply rooted in his childhood, as a kid growing up in public housing in Queens... He understands that education is ... the force that lifts children from public housing projects to first-generation college students..." (Duncan 2010).

In the time since Jim Crow we see two clear paths opening for African Americans: sports and music. All the 'education' in the world has not expanded the perceived paths by which whole communities have been lifted out of poverty. For this fact, people become discouraged.... people lose hope. People turn away from the traditional ways of making wealth and instead seek alternative pathways that offer a more foreseeable opportunity. Often times, these economic ventures included illegal activities which further diminished the black family.

My time standing in line for government cheese can be encapsulated in a single event. The routine of buying two dollars worth of polish sausage from our local corner store had run its course. Our family was destitute. Begging from a neighbor runs its course just as quickly in a ghetto community. Putting ends together is an arduous process. These and other factors in our Democratic-led community forced us to find food elsewhere, especially during the summer when we were not guaranteed our free school lunch. Today many Hispanic families are contending with these struggles. That is why the public school system has created special summer programs for these students which further subsidize the diets of children in poverty. The federal government pays for these programs because these children need to master English. They are not-native speakers and receive additional funding based purely on this fact. Native English speakers who are impoverished do not benefit from summer services unless they qualify by falling into some federally-determined classification, such as those fifth graders who failed the standardized testing. In other words, black children are not automatically given the subsidies other children are receiving from the public education fund. But if they fail, the qualify. Even at the youngest of ages, blacks are encouraged to fail by the system who pays them more, in the way of subsidies, when they do.

In my day, this was true. During summer months we had to find food elsewhere. On one occasion, which I referenced earlier, we stood in the hot Atlanta sun, bellies rumbling, waiting for the sound of the locks creaking open. We had waited for hours, hoping to make sure we were first in line (food shelters run out of food in the summer months quite frequently because they are relied on more heavily during these months). I will never forget that day.

Before knowing anything about politics - the words Democrat and Republican meant nothing to me as a child, I was at the mercy of politics. What I did know, down in the pit of my soul, was that everywhere I looked were black people... and we were all poor. Years later would I recognize that the elected officials over those communities, not just in Georgia but across the nation- those politicians were Democrat.

Education has of course lifted the African American community. The challenge comes in when the comparative elevation of other ethnic communities is evaluated. Schools in impoverished communities did not compete with schools in more affluent neighborhoods in teacher salaries, per student spending, facilities, extra-curricular supplemental education. Of course, there was no comparison between the homes the children would live and attempt homework in.

The Federal Housing Authority (FHA) and Veteran's Administration (VA) both created mortgage programs that excluded blacks, forcing impoverished families to remain in the federally subsidized housing projects while white families eventually moved out. The FHA would go on to further restrict the resale of their mortgages and engage in predatory lending practices that penalized black applicants. The racially restrictive covenants that 'officially' ended in 1948 were followed by a twenty year period of unenforceable covenants and 'redlining'[11] which use race and ethnicity as a determining factor thus perpetuating

---

[11] https://www.bostonfairhousing.org/timeline/1934-1968-FHA-Redlining.html

segregation even after the Fourteenth Amendment to the Constitution.

The impact of local zoning, FHA practices, permitting in multi-family housing developments, and the continual impact of poorer performing schools all equal the furthering of racially motivated factors that punish African American communities. Blacks suffered disproportionately under their discriminatory practices, the plan of which continued systematically under the Democrat administrations of Roosevelt, Truman, Johnson, and Carter. For this period of time, blacks suffered from poorer housing conditions, lower performing schools, and stricter prison sentencing.

Yet, the whole idea of government cheese began decades before, when in 1949, the New Deal's Agricultural Act which gave the Commodity Credit Corporation authority to purchase dairy products. This government-owned corporation wanted to stabilize prices and help the American farmer. Dairy prices rose in the 1970's and the influx of government intervention into the practices of, mostly white, dairy farmers was finally activated when then President Carter poured $2 million more into the industry.

Warehouses sprung up to house the milk byproducts including the nation's famous cheese. Farmers that had struggled during the recession now had cash to burn. 500 million pounds of stock piled cheese sat waiting for someone to decide what to do with it. Hundreds of warehouses in over thirty-five states held the 'ripening' product. An USDA official reported, as the expiration date of the cheese and other dairy products came into sight, "...the cheapest and easiest thing for us to do is dump it in the ocean."

Carter's investment in the American dairy producers led to a surplus of rapidly deteriorating cheese product, all while millions of Americans, mostly black, were going hungry. It took a change in administration and a new President for the USDA to find a solution to the moldy cheese stockpile. In December 1981, Ronald Reagan, a man who had been criticized for wanting to end welfare waste, began handing out the salvageable cheese to poor families around the nation. 30 million of the 500 million pounds of government cheese started shipping to local distribution centers around the country. Reagan created Temporary Assistance for Needy Families (TANF), a program that still distributes food today, as the country began distributing to not just needy families but also to the nation's elderly.

By and by, 300 million pounds of cheese were distributed over the course of Reagan's eight years in office throughout the 1980's. Cheese prices rescinded in the 1990's and the American government again began stockpiling cheese under the Clinton and Obama administration. Currently, there are 1.39 billion pounds of surplus cheese being stored in government owned warehouses. President Trump and Secretary of Agriculture Sonny Perdue, both Republicans, are planning to offset dairy loses by providing subsidies to China,

Canada, and Europe.[12] This translates into a $11 billion outlay by the Commodity Credit Corporation.

The icing on the cheesecake is a salty one, unfortunately. The $11 billion that will be paid to dairy farmers over the next several years, according to Progressive Dairy, a free, online and print industry specific news magazine with a reach throughout the Americas published in English, French, and Spanish, will disperse its funds over a 90% white farm base. In other words, when Democrats held the highest office in the land, white dairy farmers received government bailouts. Impoverished people living in urban centers received the surplus of cheese when Republicans took office.

Liberals and ne're-do-wells criticize the idolatry of Reagan, who oversaw the

---

[12] https://www.history.com/news/government-cheese-dairy-farmers-reagan

economic boom in the 1980's. However, in the case of government cheese, Reagan disbursed government purchased milk products, including cheese, stockpiled by Democrats at an enormous cost. Yes, the often stale and moldy cheese product often resulted in cases of constipation and embarrassment - the blue sterile stamp from the USDA on the plain cardboard box reminding the consumer of their impoverished status - but it made the best of a bad situation and provided staple meals to millions.

Many recall gub-ment cheese fondly, in retrospect. Thinking about the grilled cheese sandwiches the substance worked best for brings back memories. Especially for a family that did not qualify for other subsidy programs under TANF like Food Stamps, government cheese was a welcomed necessity. The hard block was a durable, and long lasting meal substitute, which is evidenced by how long the Department of Agriculture stored the product.

The American relationship with cheese, of any kind, in undeniable. Cheese makes everything taste better. Cheese is both the garnish and 'meat' of many meals. Government cheese was something my brother and I could make a meal out of by ourselves. In a way, it was ideal for the latch key kids growing up in ghettos all over the nation. Surprising to note that the stockpile amassed 500 million pounds of it before anyone decided to hand it out to needy children. 500 million pounds, which includes the approximately 200 million pounds that went to waste, is enough for every family in the country to have more than 2 pounds each in 2019.

During the two times in American history when government cheese was stockpiled, more than 12 million people were affected by famine and drought worldwide. Since 1964, the American government has spent in excess of $100 million per year on food stamps all while it stockpiles food for no declared or apparent reason other than to supply farmers with contracts to keep producing.

The Bottom Line

- Surplus food programs provided many needy families with the necessary staples to survive.
- Throughout history, these surplus foods have been stockpiled by the United States government at a cost of millions of dollars to taxpayers.
- Presidents Carter, Clinton, and Obama were in office when millions of pounds of surplus food wasted away in government warehouses.
- White farmers were paid, despite the waste, for producing the surplus foods.

Gentrification

There are two definitions of gentrification that, while similar, do have a distinctly different motive as to why change is taking place.

Photo Credit Matthew T Rader

The most common definition is "the process of renovating and improving housing or a district so that it conforms to middle-class taste." The second definition, which I took from Wiki, is "the process of changing the character of a neighborhood or community through the influx of more affluent residents and businesses."

In either case, the resulting barrier to affordable housing always falls on the same demographic. Here's a personal tale about gentrification that began generations ago in the south. Democrat-run Georgia and many other southern states built government housing projects for predominantly white family in and around city centers. This was done to provide these families who relied on pedestrian or public transportation the relative proximity to goods and services they needed to survive. Many of these housing projects were centered around a local school that provided outreach and education to the children within walking distance of the school house. Within a generation, these families were taking advantage of low-interest housing loans that were targeted to them. They moved from the housing projects to surrounding neighborhoods in small plot, small footprint housing. Home ownership occurred, in many cases, within one generation. As the white families moved out of thee projects, black families moved in.

Legislation that came after separate but equal made sure that whites had a clear path out of the projects so that blacks could be contained in them. Blacks who resisted the low-income convenience of housing project life took advantage of other government programs like Section 8 of the Housing and Urban Development (HUD) code and moved to concentrated communities in designated areas.

My grandmother lived in a housing project within eyeshot of the State Capitol in Georgia. Like many families around her, they developed lives and communities in their surroundings. It became home.

The families and neighbors we grew up knowing had lived in the same building or unit for generations. In fact, the community was multi-generational overall. In the 1950's, these apartments provided access to indoor plumbing, sanitation, education, and a host of modern conveniences, like having a grocery store within walking distance. As previously mentioned, there was also access to medical facilities and transportation. These improvements, while appearing basic if not substandard, were hugely critical to black economic development post Jim Crow.

In states throughout the south, that had been previously agrarian, most descendants of former slaves still lived in rural areas. They farmed or work for home-based businesses, but there was no clear path for entire communities to raise out of poverty; no clear path without access to education and public services. That was one benefit of people moving to the cities and living in government subsidized housing. For many, however, project life became more than a stepping stone in real-estate acquisition. Project life became a new way of experiencing diminished dreams, complacency, and broken families.

Trapped in the urban decay of the 1970's, 80's, and 90's meant that families living in government housing projects were at ground zero for drug and gang activity, and other kinds of violence. A generation into project life, the majority of low income blacks, which accounted for nearly 99% of blacks living in urban centers, had made few inroads into accumulating what would be described as wealth. The learning curve, if you will, from farm to board room was exhaustive. Schools in these communities were not equipped to handle the full load of onboarding needed to expose these communities to the tools and tricks of the trade needed to be competitive. The wage earning gap between whites and blacks continued to widen even as blacks acquired the basic necessities.

When legal barriers to voting, employment, education, and other civilities were eliminated, politicians and investors had to create other ways to segregate consumers. One such practice, "contract for deed" was the focus of a recent study under the aid of The Contract Buyers League, the Samuel Dubois Center on Social Equality based out of Duke University, and local housing activists in Chicago, where the study was based. With many interviews caught on film, areas like Trumball Park in Chicago were called the 'Shame of the Nation.'

In these communities, forced integration took place. Some black families jumped at the chance to be put in harm's way in exchange for better housing for their families. Under the economic programs of Democratic President Franklin D. Roosevelt, families needing relief after the Great Depression were moved into government subsidized housing projects commissioned by the local housing authority. When black families moved into these predominantly white projects, they endured a constant barrage of insults, threats, and riotous violence from their new neighbors. Trumball Park was no different. When leaving the community, blacks required a police escort to ensure their safety. This was the case throughout the nation until the white families began moving out. But blacks who endured the racist onslaught would have been in a position to take advantage of the same housing loans as white if further escalation had not been introduced.

Another change in policy

Blacks were not deterred by the threats of whites living in housing projects thanks in part to the Voting Rights and the Civil Rights Act. By 1970, blacks had taken over the housing projects. In an effort to help white families move out of the projects in the two decades following World War II, a process of predatory lending practices known as redlining was instituted by government backed loans.

Lenders argued that integration resulted in such violence that the Federal Housing Authority (FHA) could not, in the interest of domestic tranquility, back loans in mixed-race communities. This process, called redlining, effectively kept blacks from participating in the housing boom that eventually followed. In order to move through the projects into single family housing, blacks entered into 'contract for deed' negotiations with investors willing to make a profit from black sweat equity.

The outcome of these kind of dark negotiations, which took place from 1950 until the 1970's, is that black families were effectively up-charged on mortgage payments to the tune of 3.2 billion in Chicago alone. Interest rates, monthly maintenance, frequent evictions and defaults on property for one single missed payment, and other predatory practices such as a lack of equity left black families without the means to accumulate wealth, take advantage of low interest rates on conventional loans, or reinvestment into their own communities. In the Chicago study, researchers affirmed that most real estate agents were white, as were the investors who profited from the discriminatory practices, resulting in a direct wealth transfer based on ethnicity.

After the 1970's these unfair housing practices continued. The climate was marked by indiscriminate federal lending, widespread foreclosures, inflated home values, and outright corruption. The FHA scandal at HUD was documented in 1973 in a book entitled Cities Destroyed for Cash. While racial disparages dwindled in education, healthcare, and employment, housing was the one illusive commodity that kept black families from gaining the kind of wealth that meant future generations could build on the hard work of their ancestors. Let's face it, home ownership is one of the steadiest means of passing on wealth in our Republic. Without a means to do so, many black families continued to rent, even as they moved north during the Great Migration. Home ownership remained a chimerical American Dream for African Americans.

However, gentrification is more than just the corrupt lending practices of racist financiers, realtors, and investors. Gentrification involves the displacement and purchasing of traditionally minority communities at below market value. Many of the homes blacks did finally gain ownership of after Jim Crow became dilapidated over the years. Reinvestment in these communities was nonexistent. The homes were worth less than the land they sat on. This caused an influx of investors to buy up these homes and displace entire groups of people. What is not typically discussed in this process is the social-emotional impact of gentrification.

Many African Americans experienced the loss of identity through slavery. The practice not only separated families and cultures, it also separated people from purpose. Africa is a continent predominantly strengthened by their mineral rights as well as agriculture and aquaculture. In their season of bondage, these same slaves worked the land or the coastal areas to produce crops as they did back in the mother continent which were in turn captured by their masters as they had once been. Their identity became legally tied to their ability to produce and yield their produce to their 'masters.' Unruly, sick, disabled, or otherwise unproductive slaves were of less value. Their identity, if you will, was determined based on their ability to bring the master wealth - not in their innate value as people. After the Civil War, the same was true. Legal freedom did not equal economic freedom; and in some ways, still has not helped blacks overcome the traumas of false or inadequate identity.

In many schools today, teachers will still tell black children that they are not appreciated, not valued by society. People have become burdened in society and disparages between various groups breed feelings of inadequacy. But that is why the Constitution is so flawless. It simple states that the gifts within each one of us, which the Bible states are 'without repentance,' are given by our Creator. This delineation is crucial especially for people who have had their identities compromised from the trauma of slavery and are looking for validation in culture.

Gentrification, which is an economic practice, added insult to the injury African Americans experienced in slavery. When formerly ethnic communities were bought up and sold to the highest bidder for economic gain, the centers of the communities were displaced as well. In other words, when free blacks created safe spaces for themselves post Jim Crow, gentrification destroyed those centers for economic gain of those who resembled the 'masters' of the past. But how do politicians factor into this practice? The answer is quite sinister.

To use an example, close to home, I'll shed some light on the West End are of Atlanta, Georgia. After Jim Crow, blacks who sought home ownership and opportunity outside of government housing projects were funnelled into one or two specific areas of town that had been pre-determined by racist city planners. One of these communities was called the West End. This community saw expansive growth in community, small business, and in housing. Blacks prospered in this area and established themselves in concentrated centers. What was unknown to them during this urban migration was the fact that city planners, zoning officials, builders, and investors had already determined to make sure that the superstructure of these communities were inherently limited.

Strategic road closures, permitting, and construction loans were all utilized to limit the amount of growth blacks could accomplish and the amount of state of county funding they could receive. Even outside of this, public transportation was limited in these communities as were the ability to receive certain services, such as trash pick up, high speed cable or wi-fi, mall expansion and other advances. As the population grew, the community suffered from overcrowding and societal ills caused by an influx of people without economic opportunity.

Now in the West End, most houses are dilapidated, empty, already condemned. The neighborhoods are ripe for gentrification. While many look to the developers as the enemy of the community, but in fact, it is the city planners that kept economic growth from naturally occurring through free markets that is the true enemy.

The Bottom Line

- Blacks still suffer from the loss of positive self-identification.
- Gentrification is an economic practice, not a social practice.
- City planners created opportunities for gentrification by limiting the natural economic growth that can take place in a community.
- Most communities that suffer from gentrification have been run by black Democratic politicians for generations. Prior to these black overseers being

elected, white Democrats laid the foundation for systematically limiting these communities through strategically racial permitting and zoning.

Gerrymandering

The Lord said to her, "Two nations are in your womb, and two peoples from within you will be separated; one people will be stronger than the other, and the older will serve the younger."

~ Genesis 25:23

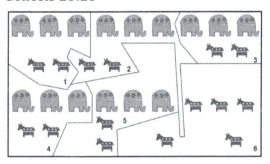

Photo Credit The Progressive Cynic

People who originated in Africa began a global exodus long before European and British smugglers brought them to the American continent as slaves. While this is unknown to most, there is evidence that Africans were living in the middle east prior to the Suez Canal dividing the African continent from the Asian continent at Egypt through an isthmus, which is a narrow land bridge separating two countries.

The importance of Suez with regard to gerrymandering was part of a migration of people that began generations ago. Construction on the canal began in 1859 and was opened in 1869. However, historians point to great Pharaohs of old who may have started connecting the Sea of Suez (the Red Sea as it is historically known) to the Nile. Around 1850 BCE, a irrigation channel stretching along the 75 mile stretch of land which made navigation easier during the flood season.

Aristotle wrote that King Darius stopped ancient construction on the canal lest sea water mix with the river and spoil it. Ptolemy II was said to have made the trench that would later be called the Suez Canal 100 feet wide by 30 feet deep. A twelfth dynasty Egyptian Pharaoh Sesostris, Necho II of the 26th dynasty, and Ramesses II all took part in extending the canal according to Greek historians and French cartographers. In short, until the great Pharaohs of Egypt began construction on diving the African continent from the Asian subcontinent for maritime ease, black people were freely able to navigate across thousands of miles on foot without obstruction. In fact, due to the great wealth of Egypt, darker skinned people would have traveled on the Silk Road as far as the Pacific Ocean on one side, as far south as the Indian ocean and all parts in between, to the Atlanta Ocean on the West coast of Africa.

The Babylonian, Ottoman, Byzantine, and British Empires all made claims to these lands. But the migration of people of color was never hindered based on political boundaries. Egypt's wealth, especially under the six female Pharaohs that ruled Egypt: Merneith, Nefertiti, Hatshepsut, Neferusobek, Tawosret, and Cleopatra,[13] was unprecedented giving people of color a global level of wealth which was carried throughout the continent as people migrated East and West. Eventually, large numbers of black men settled coastal villages all around Africa's ports.

Once Africa was officially cut off from Asia by land, it ended the path of foot migration that had been realized by people in the region for more than a thousand years.

The settlement of Suez had less than 4,000 inhabitants prior to the construction of the canal. During construction, populations grew to tens of thousands peasants who came to provide manpower to the construction project. Originally condemned

---

[13]

https://www.nationalgeographic.com/culture/2018/11/kara-cooney-queens-of-egypt-women-rule-the-world/

by the British government, the Suez Canal Company was jointly owned by French and Egyptian interests. When Egyptian ruler I. Pasha ended forced labor on the project, steam and coal powered dredgers finished the job. When Egypt struggled financially, Britain eventually bought 44% of Egyptian shares in the project. The Great Bitter Lake, the mid-point of this stretch of sea, was the temporary home to a fleet of 15 international ships which were blocked by the Egyptian government. This act by Egypt was part of the Six Days War, now referred to as the Arab-Israeli War Egypt, Jordan, and Syria fought with Israel in 1967. Ultimately, Israel won the war and regained their ancient lands.

Both Arab and Israeli residents sought access to their Holy Lands and respective sights, But it was Israel who, after much controversy, returned the Golan Heights to Syria and the Gaza Strip to Egypt in exchange for peace agreements. Conflicts initiated by Egypt along the Suez Canal continued throughout the 1960's. Full withdrawal of Israel troops from Gaza did not occur until 2005. In other words, the conflicts caused in the region have been exasperated by fights of the land and the waterways for decades.

It is easy to suggest that the building of the Suez Canal, Arab-Israeli conflicts, and peace negotiations in the Middle East have little to do with African Americans and this whole idea of gerrymandering. However, the residential and settlement patterns of black people can be traced back to the continent of Africa. Africans have resettled across the continent at will until the interventions of other nations who have fought over the land, and the waterways, limiting access to these lands and redistributing without full consideration of cultural implications, thereby limiting the political, economic, and logistical expanse of the people. This is the gist of what gerrymandering is.

When you look at the diagram above, you see that the way in which the separation dividing the 6 districts or towns, if you will, gives a seemingly unfair advantage to one group over another.

There are 15 of each kind of animal pictured above, 15 elephants and 15 donkeys. If the major has the power, then the way the lines are drawn to separate the towns or regions should take into consideration the people who already live there. Based on the lines drawn above, 5 out of the 6 districts are ruled by the "elephant" because there are more elephants than there are donkeys. District 6 is controlled by the "donkeys" because the majority of people who live there belong to this group. Many believe that, like this picture suggests, Republicans, pictured as the elephant, have drawn the lines (called redistricting) to increase their power and diminish the power of the Democrats, pictured as the donkey.

The problem with that theory is that Democrat controlled Congress, just as Republican controlled state legislatures, each have the opportunity to draw or redraw the lines based on the migration of people. As pictured above, and based on the ancient migration patterns in Africa, blacks have a tendency to self-segregate themselves into dense 'cultural centers' in which, as pictured above in section 6, their numbers do not yield the same level of power as they would if they had spread out. Even though both donkeys and elephants are the same in population, elephants have the power because they outnumber the donkeys in 5 out of 6 districts.

The problem with this theory is that you could divide this same group of animals into a variety of groupings and you would still have the same results: elephants in charge. Why is that? Because most of the donkeys all live near each other. This pattern of self segregating started, perhaps, way back hundreds of years ago with the first attempts at building the canal at Suez, in Egypt. Being cut off from a region became the norm after generations of having others define their living space. By choosing to segregate in advance of those in political or economic control demanding a forced migration gives people, especially black people, a chance to

- exercise free will without fear of annexation,
- reinforce the idea of self determination,
- propagandize the theory of gerrymandering, and
- all cultural centers to develop without interruption.

While three of these outcomes are considered positive, the fourth, a negative outcome, is necessary to categorize the phenomenon as worthy of discussion. But those who accuse Republicans, primarily, of gerrymandering are the same who admit that the compact housing patterns of blacks and browns pose a considerable challenge to redistricting. However, when Democrats hold power, do they not also redraw political boundaries as needed? Of course they do. The question is, how much is too much redistricting? And is there irrefutable proof that decisions made with regard to redistricting are made with race as the foremost determining factor. I redrew the map above five difference ways and it still ended up the elephants as the people of power due to the high concentration of donkeys in the southeast corner of the diagram.

The accusation of gerrymandering, an unethical practice named after Edbridge Gerry, a Democrat Governor from Massachusetts, has drawn legal action from time to time. As of the printing of this book, there are over twelve cases of gerrymandering being brought against the Secretary of State of each respective state. While there may be some credence in a few of these cases, the Brennan Center of Justice at NYU School of Law, a leading policy institution founded in memory of Supreme Court Justice William J. Brennan, Jr., only identified four key cases in which a clear case of racial or partisan gerrymandering could be proven.

Racial Gerrymandering

The practice of redrawing congressional districts every ten years to coincide with the decennial census is common legislative practice. Districts that grow rapidly may opt to redistrict in between the decennial census - in these instances, a gerrymander is more likely. That is why many states have selected an independent redistricting commission to ensure that racial and political gerrymandering does not occur. On the occasion that an accusation of gerrymander on these grounds has been made, legal action can ensue. Most cases of racial gerrymander, however, ended in the Jim Crow south.

Southern Democrats did more to oppress the vote based on race than any other group. In fact, Democrats along the eastern seaboard can be linked to cases of voter suppression through gerrymandering, or biased redistricting, even after the Voter Rights Amendment was passed.

In 1995, the Supreme Court heard the case of Miller v. Johnson in Georgia. At the time, Democrat liberal Zell Miller was Governor and fellow Democrat Lewis Massey served as Secretary of State. Ultimately, the court found in favor of the plaintiff, indicating the Georgia's redistricting plan violated the

Equal Protection Clause of the Fourteenth Amendment. The question before the court had been whether or not racial gerrymandering of the congressional districts fell under the Equal Protection Clause of the 14th. Justice Anthony Kennedy wrote the majority opinion stating, "a reapportionment plan may be so highly irregular and bizarre in shape that it rationally cannot be understood as anything other than an effort to segregate voters based on race." Justice Kennedy cited Shaw v. Reno (1993) which stated that if race is the overriding and predominant force (or benefactor) of the redistricting, then Equal Protection has been violated.

The state earned an additional district due to a population boom. The case was brought by white voters who identified the abnormal shape of the proposed district racially favored one group over another. Since the district was found in violation, new districts had to be identified that passed the gerrymander rule of thumb.

Shaw v. Reno (1993) was part of the landmark set of cases that contributed to the Voting Rights Act of 1965. In the 2000 census, a majority-black district was identified in North Carolina, in order to improve black representation. However, Justice Sandra Day O'Connor, when delivering the majority opinion, held that the new district could only be described as "political apartheid" because the new boundaries clearly identified black neighborhoods throughout the central part of the state to form a new district (indicated in pink below).

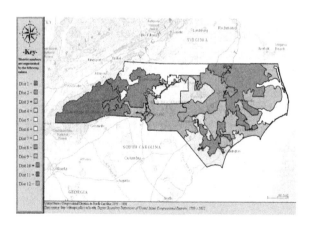

Photo Credit US Department of the Interior (public domain)

Like in the Georgia case, the Supreme Court upheld the case brought in Shaw v. Reno and the District had to be redrawn. Again, white voters brought the case before the accusation as Shaw v. Barr (1992). The final holding in the case was "Redistricting based on race must be held to a standard of strict scrutiny under the equal protection clause while bodies doing redistricting must be conscious of race to the extent that they must ensure compliance with the Voting Rights Act."

Like the Democrat for which the term is named, gerrymandering has been used by Democrats throughout history to create racially segregated districts which unconstitutionally violate the Equal Protection Clause of the Fourteenth Amendment as well as the Voting Rights Act of 1965.

Partisan Gerrymandering

Far more likely than racial gerrymandering in modern times, partisan gerrymandering is the redistricting for the purposes of providing an advantage to a particular party. Again, census data taken every decade is supposed to be the driving force behind redistricting. However, depending on what party is in power at the time of the census, election results can impact the outcome of any plans to redistrict. This, in mind, a bi-partisan effort to reduce partisan gerrymandering is currently underway in Congress being led by Senator Whitehouse and former Senator John McCain. Princeton University researchers state that partisan gerrymandering is a systematic problem in that both major parties do it. [14] Based on the preponderance of evidence analyzed of 2012 election cycle, only 5 states were found to have gerrymandered districts: Arizona, Michigan, North Carolina, Pennsylvania, and Wisconsin.

14

http://election.princeton.edu/2012/12/30/gerrymanders-part-1-busting-the-both-sides-do-it-myth/

In each of these five states, Republicans hold more congressional seats with, on average, less than 1% difference in voter turnout. What does this mean in practical terms? With almost 50/50 voter turnout between the Democrat and Republican parties, Republicans captured 20-50% more congressional seats (in four of the five states) as a result of redistricting.

"As an example, consider Colorado. There, 51.4% of the two-party vote went to Republican candidates, and 4 out of 7 representatives will be Republicans. Colorado's delegation therefore represents its partisans fairly."

Conversely, as in the case of Pennsylvania, Democrats received 50.7% of the vote but only 5 congressmen. While Republicans received 49.3% of the vote but earned 13 congressmen. This is an indication that either the districts are gerrymandered, or, and more unlikely, that candidates in Pennsylvania drew more swing voters from opposing parties by a margin of 2:1. In this same article, a top offender list of gerrymandered states was revealed. Six of the nine were Republican controlled, supporting the assertion that both parties gerrymander for partisan gain. Based on this data, Republican controlled states have committed more offenses.

The Partisan Voting Index (PVI or CPVI) is a measurement of how a district leans, either right or left, which is managed by the Cook Political Report, a nonpartisan online newsletter founded in 1984. Charlie Cook was a political analyst and forecaster who worked previously for the Democrat Party before beginning his own publication. PVI uses terms like Solid Democrat, Solid Republican, Lean Democrat and Lean Republican to characterize voters. However, in the 2018 midterm elections, there were 36 Republican-leaning districts represented by Democrats. This outcome indicates that majority voting is still valid means of attaining equal representation in voting. In the same vein, there are three Democratic-leaning states that elected Republican Governors.

As former President Barack Obama said in a commercial supporting The National Democratic Redistricting Committee, "most Americans are (straddling) the middle." If this is true, then cases like the recent Supreme Court decision regarding Virginia State House gerrymandering accusations, should be few and far between. The use of independent redistricting committees assist legislators in providing equality for all voters, without fear of economic retribution due to diminished or suppressed votes.

The Bottom Line

- Racial gerrymandering is illegal. Political gerrymandering must be eliminated.
- Prior to 1965, Democrats routinely created gerrymandered districts in order to suppress votes of African Americans.

- Since 1965, most cases brought to the Supreme Court with accusations of gerrymandering have been brought against Democrat Governors.
- Political gerrymandering has occurred in both parties, but more so in the Republican party in recent years.

So Now, What?

For I know the plans I have for you, says the Lord, plans to prosper you and give you a future.

Jeremiah 29:11

Photo Credit Lubo Minar

President Barack Obama had a great opportunity to level the playing field for African Americans. Whether he was kept from carrying out the plans he had or he had no plans at all, African Americans experienced higher levels of unemployment, longer criminal sentences aside from the Clinton years, and more dependency on social services during his administration. But while this book is not meant to criticize Barack Obama, it is meant to highlight the post-Obama changes that have been made in favor of the black people in this country.

First things first. Our country is a Republic, not a democracy. When we look at the definition of these two terms we will see obvious similarities. However, there are clear differences that must be pointed out. A democracy, according to Webster's dictionary, is a form of government by the people for the people in which the supreme power is vested in the people themselves. A free electoral system is part of a democracy. In a democracy, the people have certain rights and privileges. A republic, on the other hand, is a form of government in which the power resides in citizens who are entitled to vote. Upon voting for elected officials, powers are carried out by these representatives. The difference is very slight but it is a significant one.

In America, we vote. To qualify to vote you must reach a certain again of accountability, or perceived responsibility, which is currently eighteen years of age. Criteria number two is that a potential voter much also register your address with the voting bureau as well as your citizenship which is then recorded for vote calculations during the election cycle. Within the voting process, certain other parameters are set in place including the need to prove one's identity, show up to vote on a specified day and in a specified location, and the candidates themselves follow rules to be placed on the ballot. In a democracy, none of these 'rules' are in place. Democracy is simply majority rule. There are no requirements for citizenship, age restrictions, or candidate rules and regulations. In a democracy, you can theoretically change leadership every week because the if the people change their minds, then the group's leadership changes.

While some people may interchange the words democracy and republic, we can look to not only our founding documents but also to the Pledge of Allegiance we all grew up reciting. We are one Nation, under God and our flag stands for a Republic. That is the oath every citizen takes. The founding fathers went to great lengths to ensure that our country was not simply a majority rule. James Madison began this debate in Federalist No. 10, when he described the pitfalls of a simple democracy. The word democracy is not located in any of our founding documents. And while our Republic is a representative democracy, it is the key word 'representative' in which the electoral college and process of voting makes the difference. Second President of the United States, John Adams, reminded constituents that ours was not a democracy and he was close enough to the original few men who created this government and drafted our founding documents.

Huffington post CEO Gerry Myers[15] says American is not a democracy because we are not majority rule. But he also contends that while we were intended to be a Republic, we no longer are because of the corruption in Washington, DC., which yields power to large corporations and special interest groups. To that Point there is some validity. Private enterprise and capitalism is the greatest way to bring wealth to a people. Yet when there is widespread corruption, capitalism falters. The middle class desperately needs to revive the entrepreneurial spirit of America's past in order to allow the Constitution to work for all people. While it is great that our current administration has been able to achieve the lowest black unemployment rate in a generation, if middle class blacks do not own and operate businesses in their own communities we will never see and end to

---

[15] https://www.huffpost.com/entry/what-is-america-a-republi_b_6416872

the economic disparages that have plagued black America since the Reconstruction Era. Immediately following the Civil War, more black owned businesses were started in any period of American history. Black wealth skyrocketed when slavery ended and blacks began distributing their new found wealth within their own communities, initially, and ultimately through the east coast.

Yet, low black unemployment rates are not the only records President Trump has broken during his first term in office. Female unemployment has recently hit all time lows. Unemployment among veterans is also low. In 2019, $59 billion in exports grew our GDP and median household income has risen to the highest levels ever.

While President Trump is criticized daily in the media due to his crassness, no one can argue with the businessman on the 4 million jobs created. 400 thousand of those openings were manufacturing jobs that are the lifeblood of many low to middle class

Americans, many of whom are black. In the past 20 years, many manufacturing jobs went overseas due to high corporate taxes, insurance, regulation, and the minimum wage. This caused many uncolleged workers to become unemployed. Removing the individual mandate from the Affordable Care Act (Obama Care) also saved families money every month. Based on the record performance of the NY Stock Exchange, President Trump lowering taxes, cutting regulation on larger businesses, and flat out confidence has brought economic prosperity back to America, and with them, employment opportunity.

While no one would argue that Donald Trump is your average Republican, what you can clearly surmise based on the evidence in this book is that the Republican Party was founded as a result of the fight to end slavery. Since its founding, the Democrat Party has leaned far more left - catapulting its message of racism beyond the party of old which was in partnership with the Ku Klux Klan. Now Dems have disrobed and are using prominent blacks to carry on their message of economic slavery and abortion. The Blexit movement and others like it are attempting to "awaken" generational Democrats to the truth of what the party actually stands for:

1. Abortion on demand, especially if you are black or hispanic.
2. Institute socialist practices like "free" healthcare. Since nothing is free all this really means if that everyone gets a smaller piece of mediocre healthcare and must hope and pray nothing serious happens to them.
3. Cancel all college loan debt. While this is nice for people who are struggling under the debt of a higher education, it does not inspire anyone to work to pay off their own debt. Let me ask you, are you willing to pay for someone else's child to go to college? If this seems like a problem to you, please know, it's a problem for everyone!
4. Remove the right to legally own a gun. Why is this necessary to state. Because the Democrats have no plan to remove illegal gun ownership. How is it better

when only criminals and the government has guns?

5. Give illegal immigrants the same rights as natural born citizens. Every illegal immigrant costs the American taxpayers in each state about 17,800,000,000 a year in (1) education, (2) healthcare, (3) unclaimed taxes, (4) social services, (5) shared public resources, and a myriad of other expenses. Not to mention the costs, illegal immigrants "jump in line" ahead of tens of thousand of legal immigrants who follow our laws and apply for citizenship. If you wanted to become a Canadian citizen, do you think it is wrong for them to ask you to apply? Or should anyone be able to go anywhere with no regard for national sovereignty?

6. Expand government to provide for greater social services. The Democrat Party continues to throw taxpayer money at problems they have not been able to fix. President Trump has continually donated his own salary to fight the opioid addiction. This fight costs the taxpayer no additional funds

to battle one of our nation's largest problems.

Let's face it. Many in our nation are hooked on something just because self-medicating has become a cultural way of life. Pharmaceutical companies and insurance agencies have been taking advantage of loopholes in our tax system that both Democrats and Republicans have turned a blind eye to. Even though our nation is based on the principles of Judaism and Christianity, legislators have forced ungodly regulation on families, churches, and other organizations regarding the lifestyle choices of a relative few in our nation. Drugs, jail, and drive-by's haven't even come close to the number of black men eradicated by abortion. The family has been decimated. Not just black families, either. Media attacks on masculinity, free speech, and a having a difference of opinion have created a 'cold' civil war, exchanged with harsh words instead of bullets. At the center of this mess is President Trump, a man who insights patriotism as much as he insights fury just by being himself.

Nevertheless, I urge everyone who is reading this to put President Trump out of your mind. Whether you love him or hate him is irrelevant to the truth that the Republican Party, as flawed as it is, was meant for the economic freedom of all citizens, especially black citizens. Note that the 'party of Lincoln' is still the Republican Party. Understand that many Democrats have not bettered their cities, instead they have allowed greed to cloud their judgement and in turn, hurt their own people. Check the facts for yourself regarding the way abortion has decimated the black family, all with the blessing of the Democrat Party.

As I recently tweeted, racist Republicans and racist Dems are in the same party. It is true that some people who called themselves Republicans are slanted towards racism. They are Republicans in name only (RINOs) who deserve exposure. RINOs should not be a reason why any person, of any color or creed, assumes that all Republicans are racist. The platform does not support it, neither do most of the voters. A few bigots on either end of the spectrum do not a party make. But Democrats have systematically targeted blacks and therein lies the problem.

For generations, black people have voted Democrat because Momma or Daddy did. Blacks have historically voted Democrat because early Civil Rights leaders worked with the Democrats in power because they had to. Blacks and now Hispanics have voted Democrat because the new party of socialism spreads propaganda that causes people to make emotional decisions, not logical ones. Blacks vote Democrats because they have met a RINO and wrongly believe they represent all Republicans. Blacks need to take back the Republican Party for their children, and children's children.

Black people need to stand up and leave the Democrat economic propaganda plantation. We need to look past the RINOs and read the facts about both parties. We need to see the impact Democrat leadership has had on our communities. We need to stop focusing on President Trump, the person, and instead focus on the change in America. We need to understand that many blacks were better off in the 1800's than they are now because they owned property, businesses, and understood which elected officials were working with them, not against them. We need to find within ourselves a new kind of black power, one that is based on unity, not division.

America is the only nation that fought a war to end slavery. Out of that war came the Republican Party. It was the party for the freed slaves, and their descendants. Now illegal immigrants outnumber the descendants of slaves and are changing the narrative for our people. This Black History Bible isn't just about the past, it is about the future. To change the corruption, confusion, and collusion between the Democrat Party, the media, and organizations like Planned Parenthood, we need people to hear the truth, acknowledge it as truth, and tell a friend.

The Bottom Line

1. The Democrat Party has spent a lot of time, money, and talent to deceive black people out of their votes.
2. They use other black people to spread the message of racism.
3. Republicans in name only (RINOs) do not represent the values of the Republican Party.
4. The Republican Party was founded to end slavery, slavery of all kinds.
5. The only way to change the damage done to our community is for black voices to rise up in truth - in politics by running for office or by casting a vote for politicians who are fighting socialism.
6. Stop focusing on the negative feelings you may have toward President Trump or any other Republican for that matter. Look at the facts instead.

7. Face the facts that blacks are being targeted and the most powerful weapon we have is our vote. Friends don't let friends vote irresponsibly.

The Healing

The only way for the descendents of slaves to shake off the bounds of economic slavery we currently find ourselves in, we must look beyond the emotional woundings of the past and look toward the future. The future is in our vote.

The following resources are available from usa.gov

Who Can and Who Can't

Who Can and Can't Vote in U.S. Elections

You must be a U.S. citizen to vote in federal, state or local elections.

Who Can Vote?

You can vote in U.S. elections if you:

- Are a U.S. citizen
- Meet your state's residency requirements
- [You can be homeless](#) and still meet these requirements.
- Are 18 years old on or before Election Day
- In some states, you can register to vote before you turn 18 if you will be 18 by Election Day.
- Are registered to vote by your state's voter registration deadline. North Dakota does not require voter registration.

Who CAN'T Vote?

- Non-citizens, including permanent legal residents
- Some people with felony convictions. Rules vary by state. Check with your state elections office about the laws in your state.
- Some people who are mentally incapacitated. Rules vary by state.
- For President in the general election: U.S. citizens residing in U.S. territories

Check with your state or local election office for any questions about who can and cannot vote.

Your First Time?

First Time Voters

In addition to the laws governing what identification all voters must show at the polls, first time voters may face additional requirements. The federal Help America Vote Act ([section 15483(b)(2)(A)](#)) mandates that all states require identification from first-time voters who register to vote by mail and have not provided verification of their identification at the time of registration. The act lists a "current and valid photo identification" or "a copy of a current utility bill, bank statement, government check, paycheck, or other government document that shows the name and address of the voter" as acceptable forms of ID.

Exceptions to Voter Identification Requirements

Most states with strict voter identification requirements make some exceptions. Including exceptions from laws that both are and are not in place for 2016. These exceptions may include people who:

- Have religious objections to being photographed (Arkansas, Indiana, Kansas, Mississippi, South Carolina, Tennessee, Texas, Wisconsin)
- Are indigent (Indiana, Tennessee)
- "Have a reasonable impediment" to getting an ID (South Carolina)
- Do not have an ID as a result of a recent natural disaster (Texas)
- People who are victims of domestic abuse, sexual assault or stalking and have a "confidential listing" (Wisconsin)

Additionally, voter ID requirements generally apply to in-person voting, not to absentee ballots or mailed ballots.

All voters, regardless of the type of verification required by the states, are subject to perjury charges if they vote under false pretenses.

Preamble Left

In 2016, Democrats meet in Philadelphia with the same basic belief that animated the Continental Congress when they gathered here 240 years ago: Out of many, we are one. Under President Obama's leadership, and thanks to the hard work and determination of the American people, we have come a long way from the Great Recession and the Republican policies that triggered it. American businesses have now added 14.8 million jobs since private-sector job growth turned positive in early 2010. Twenty million people have gained health insurance coverage. The American auto industry just had its best year ever. And we are getting more of our energy from the sun and wind, and importing less oil from overseas. But too many Americans have been left out and left behind. They are working longer hours with less security. Wages have barely budged and the racial wealth gap remains wide, while the cost of everything from childcare to a college education has continued to rise. And for too many families, the dream of homeownership is out of reach.

As working people struggle, the top one percent accrues more wealth and more power. Republicans in Congress have chosen gridlock and dysfunction over trying to find solutions to the real challenges we face. It's no wonder that so many feel like the system is rigged against them. Democrats believe that cooperation is better than conflict, unity is better than division, empowerment is better than resentment, and bridges are better than walls. It's a simple but powerful idea: we are stronger together. Democrats believe we are stronger when we have an economy that works for everyone—an economy that grows incomes for working people, creates good-paying jobs, and puts a middle-class life within reach for more Americans. Democrats believe we can spur more sustainable economic growth, which will create good-paying jobs and raise wages. And we can have more economic fairness, so the rewards are shared broadly, not just with those at the top.

We need an economy that prioritizes long-term investment over short-term profit-seeking, rewards the common interest over self-interest, and promotes innovation and entrepreneurship. We believe that today's extreme level of income and wealth inequality—where the majority of the economic gains go to the top one percent and the richest 20 people in our country own more wealth than the bottom 150 million—makes our economy weaker, our communities poorer, and our politics poisonous. And we know that our nation's long struggle with race is far from over. More than half a century after Rosa Parks sat and Dr. King marched and John Lewis bled, more than half a century after César Chávez, Dolores 2 Huerta, and Larry Itliong organized, race still plays a significant role in determining who gets ahead in America and who gets left behind. We must face that reality and we must fix it.

We believe a good education is a basic right of all Americans, no matter what zip code they live in. We will end the school-to-prison pipeline and build a cradle-to-college pipeline instead, where every child can live up to his or her God-given potential. We believe in helping Americans balance work and family without fear of punishment or penalty. We believe in at last guaranteeing equal pay for women. And as the party that created Social Security, we believe in protecting every American's right to retire with dignity. We firmly believe that the greed, recklessness, and illegal behavior on Wall Street must be brought to an end. Wall Street must never again be allowed to threaten families and businesses on Main Street. Democrats believe we are stronger when we protect citizens' right to vote, while stopping corporations' outsized influence in elections. We will fight to end the broken campaign finance system, overturn the disastrous Citizens United decision, restore the full power of the Voting Rights Act, and return control of our elections to the American people. Democrats believe that climate change poses a real and urgent threat to our economy, our national security, and our children's health and futures, and that Americans deserve the jobs and security that come from becoming the clean energy superpower of the 21st century. Democrats believe we are stronger and safer when

America brings the world together and leads with principle and purpose. We believe we should strengthen our alliances, not weaken them.

We believe in the power of development and diplomacy. We believe our military should be the best-trained, best-equipped fighting force in the world, and that we must do everything we can to honor and support our veterans. And we know that only the United States can mobilize common action on a truly global scale, to take on the challenges that transcend borders, from international terrorism to climate change to health pandemics. Above all, Democrats are the party of inclusion. We know that diversity is not our problem—it is our promise. As Democrats, we respect differences of perspective and belief, and pledge to work together to move this country forward, even when we disagree.

With this platform, we do not merely seek common ground—we strive to reach higher ground. We are proud of our heritage as a nation of immigrants. We know that today's immigrants are tomorrow's teachers, doctors, lawyers, government leaders, soldiers, entrepreneurs, activists, PTA members, and pillars of our communities. We believe in protecting civil liberties and guaranteeing civil rights and voting rights, women's rights and workers' rights, LGBT rights, and rights for people with disabilities. We believe America is still, as Robert Kennedy said, "a great country, an unselfish country, and a compassionate country." These principles stand in sharp contrast to the Republicans, who have nominated as the standard bearer for their party and their candidate for President a man who seeks to appeal to Americans' basest differences, rather than our better natures. The stakes have been high in previous elections. But in 2016, the stakes can be measured in human lives— 3 in the number of immigrants who would be torn from their homes; in the number of faithful and peaceful Muslims who would be barred from even visiting our shores; in the number of allies alienated and dictators courted; in the number of Americans who would lose access to health care and see their rights ripped away.

This election is about more than Democrats and Republicans. It is about who we are as a nation, and who we will be in the future. Two hundred and forty years ago, in Philadelphia, we started a revolution of ideas and of action that continues to this day. Since then, our union has been tested many times, through bondage and civil war, segregation and depression, two world wars and the threat of nuclear annihilation. Generations of Americans fought and marched and organized to widen the circle of opportunity and dignity—and we are fighting still. Despite what some say, America is and has always been great—but not because it has been perfect. What makes America great is our unerring belief that we can make it better. We can and we will build a more just economy, a more equal society, and a more perfect union—because we are stronger together.

Preamble Right

With this platform, we the Republican Party reaffirm the principles that unite us in a common purpose.

We believe in American exceptionalism.

We believe the United States of America is unlike any other nation on earth.

We believe America is exceptional because of our historic role — first as refuge, then as defender, and now as exemplar of liberty for the world to see.

We affirm — as did the Declaration of Independence: that all are created equal, endowed by their Creator with inalienable rights of life, liberty, and the pursuit of happiness.

We believe in the Constitution as our founding document.

We believe the Constitution was written not as a flexible document, but as our enduring covenant.

We believe our constitutional system — limited government, separation of powers, federalism, and the rights of the people — must be preserved uncompromised for future generations.

We believe political freedom and economic freedom are indivisible.

When political freedom and economic freedom are separated — both are in peril; when united, they are invincible.

We believe that people are the ultimate resource — and that the people, not the government, are the best stewards of our country's God-given natural resources.

As Americans and as Republicans we wish for peace — so we insist on strength. We will make America safe. We seek friendship with all peoples and all nations, but we recognize and are prepared to deal with evil in the world.

Based on these principles, this platform is an invitation and a roadmap. It invites every American to join us and shows the path to a stronger, safer, and more prosperous America.

This platform is optimistic because the American people are optimistic.

This platform lays out — in clear language — the path to making America great and united again.

For the past 8 years America has been led in the wrong direction.

Our economy has become unnecessarily weak with stagnant wages. People living paycheck to paycheck are struggling, sacrificing, and suffering.

Americans have earned and deserve a strong and healthy economy.

Our standing in world affairs has declined significantly — our enemies no longer fear us and our friends no long trust us.

People want and expect an America that is the most powerful and respected country on the face of the earth.

The men and women of our military remain the world's best. The have been shortchanged in numbers, equipment, and benefits by a Commander in Chief who treats the Armed Forces and our veterans as a necessary inconvenience.

The President and the Democrat Party have dismantled Americans' system of healthcare. They have replaced it with a costly and complicated scheme that limits choices and takes away our freedom.

The President and the Democrat Party have abandoned their promise of being accountable to the American people.

They have nearly doubled the size of the national debt.

They refuse to control our borders but try to control our schools, farms, businesses, and even our religious institutions. They have directly attacked the production of American energy and the industry-related jobs that have sustained families and communities.

The President has been regulating to death a free market economy that he does not like and does not understand. He defies the laws of the United States by refusing to enforce those with which he does not agree.

And he appoints judges who legislate from the bench rather than apply the law.

We, as Republicans and Americans, cannot allow this to continue. That is why the many sections of this platform affirm our trust in the people, our faith in their judgment, and our determination to help them take back their country.

This means removing the power from unelected, unaccountable government.

This means relieving the burden and expense of punishing government regulations.

And this means returning to the people and the states the control that belongs to them. It is the control and the power to make their own decisions about what's best for themselves and their families and communities.

This platform is many things: A handbook for returning decision-making to the people. A guide to the constitutional rights of every American. And a manual for the kind of sustained growth that will bring opportunity to all those on the sidelines of our society.

Every time we sing, "God Bless America," we are asking for help. We ask for divine help that our country can fulfill its promise. We earn that help by recommitting ourselves to the ideas and ideals that are the true greatness of America.

Election Crimes

Election Crimes

In democratic societies like the United States, the voting process is a means by which citizens hold their government accountable; conflicts are channeled into resolutions and power transfers peacefully. Our system of representative government works only when honest ballots are not diluted by fraudulent ballots. The FBI, through its Public Corruption Unit, has an important but limited role in ensuring fair and free elections. Election crimes become federal cases when:

- The ballot includes one or more federal candidates;
- The crime involves an election official abusing his duties;
- The crime pertains to fraudulent voter registration;
- Voters are not U.S. citizens.

Federal election crimes fall into three broad categories—campaign finance crimes, voter/ballot fraud, and civil rights violations.

Campaign finance

- A person gives more than $4,600 to a federal candidate (various limits apply for donations to and from committees and groups);
- A donor asks a friend to give money to a federal candidate, promising to reimburse the friend; the friend makes the donation and the real donor reimburses him;
- A corporation gives corporate money to a federal candidate;
- A person who is neither a citizen nor a green card holder gives money to a federal, state, or local candidate.

Civil rights violations

- Someone threatens a voter with physical or economic harm unless the voter casts his ballot in a particular way;
- Someone tries to prevent qualified voters from getting to the polls in a federal election;
- A scheme exists to prevent minorities from voting.

Voter/ballot fraud

- A voter intentionally gives false information when registering to vote;
- A voter receives money or something of value in exchange for voting in a federal election or registering to vote;
- Someone votes more than once in a federal election;
- An election official corrupts his or her office to benefit a candidate or party (e.g., lets unqualified voters cast ballots).

What is NOT a federal election crime:

- Giving voters a ride to the polls;
- Offering voters a stamp to mail an absentee ballot;
- Giving voters time off to vote;
- Violating state campaign finance laws;
- Distributing inaccurate campaign literature;
- Campaigning too close to the polls;
- Trying to convince an opponent to withdraw from a race.

If you think an election crime is occurring, call the election crimes coordinator at your [local FBI office.](#)

Accessibility in Voting

Several federal laws protect the voting rights of Americans with disabilities. These include the Americans with Disabilities Act (ADA) and the Help America Vote Act (HAVA).

Voters with disabilities have the right to:

- Vote in private, without help
- Have an accessible polling place with voting machines for voters with disabilities

Polling places must have:

- Wheelchair-accessible voting booths
- Entrances and doorways at least 32 inches wide
- Handrails on all stairs
- Voting equipment for people who are blind or visually impaired

If you have a disability, you may:

- Seek help from poll workers trained to use an accessible voting machine, or
- Bring someone to help you vote

You can also ask your election office what other options you have.

- Some states offer "curbside voting," when a poll worker brings everything you need to vote to your car.
- Some set up polling places at long-term care facilities.
- Local organizations may provide transportation to the polls.
- Many states let people with disabilities vote by mail.

Absentee & Early Voting

Absentee Voting

- Get your absentee ballot from your state or territory.
- Visit your state or territorial election office website and look for "Absentee Voting" or "Voting By Mail." If you don't see either term, try using the site's search tool.
- Your state may require you to have a valid excuse to vote absentee. Acceptable excuses vary by state. Most include:
- Being unable to get to your polling place due to illness, injury, or disability.
- Being on business travel or vacation outside of your county or city of residence on Election Day
- Being a student at an out-of-state college or university
- This National Conference of State Legislatures table shows which states require an excuse.

- Follow your state's instructions for requesting an absentee or vote-by-mail ballot.

Military and Overseas Voters

Early Voting

Sometimes circumstances make it hard or impossible for you to vote on Election Day. But your state may let you vote during a designated early voting period.

- Most states have early voting. This lets registered voters vote on specified dates before Election Day.
- You don't need an excuse to vote early.
- In some states, you may cast an absentee ballot in person before Election Day. To do this, you must request an absentee ballot from your state. Your state may require you to submit a valid excuse too.

Time Frames for Early Voting

This early voting chart lists time frames for states that offer early voting.

The rules change from state to state. Make sure you know yours if you plan to vote early or in-person absentee.

The best place to check is your state/territorial election office website. Check under "absentee voting" if you don't see information listed under "voting in person" or "early voting."

Teaching Patriotism

The question as to whether or not public schools should teach patriotism is still debatable in certain sectors. To what degree teaching this subject matter is Constitutional and how can successful patriotism be taught are undetermined algorithms. It's difficult enough in some neighborhoods to teach multiplication, which has an assigned, undisputed set of factors and protocols. In light of all of the absenting opinions, patriotism is not as clear cut.

In 1828, patriotism was defined as "Love of one's country; the passion which aims to serve one's country, either in defending it from invasion, or protecting its rights and maintaining its laws and institutions in vigor and purity. Patriotism is the characteristic of a good citizen, the noblest passion that animates a man in the character of a citizen." By today's definition, less than two hundred years later, patriotism is simply coined as "devoted love, support, and defense of one's country; national loyalty." Does the reduction in words come as a result of the fast paced society we now find ourselves in, or is there more to it?

The fact of it is that people define patriotism differently. What is patriotic to one person is offensive to another. The meaning behind the words we use give listeners untold number of skepticism and doubt because we have come to accept truth as being progressive, not abstract. When truth changes based on the circumstances happening at any given time, how can one clearly identify what is or is not patriotic. That is why it is so difficult for public school teachers to go deep when it comes to teaching patriotism.

With students all over the country returning to classrooms, it's time to find out exactly where we stand. The real truth is that when we spend all of our focus on what we do not agree on, we do not focus on the things we do agree on; and that's anti-patriotic.

Public schools were designed to teach immigrants pouring into this country how to be successful Americana, among other things. Horace Mann, as Secretary of

Education, proposed a standard curriculum to the Massachusetts assembly which was eventually adopted by other states. This standard curriculum was set up to reduce the disparages between the wealthy, who were able to hire teachers to education their children, and the impoverished, who were functionally illiterate in many cases. Patriotism was one of the subjects early American schools promoted. They did so not just to unify the young nation, but to help perpetuate what the nation was founded on.

The influx of other cultures were to add to the definition of 'America,' not detract from it. Public school ensured this notion of national identity from a very early point in American history.

In fact, since the early public schools, the government debated on whether or not tax payers should pick up where parents left off and to what degree. Education reforms during the civil rights era, for example, officially ended segregation in the United States. This was considered a national priority when public outcry to adhere to the Constitution's definition of citizenship won out over prejudice. The Convention Against Discrimination in Education was adopted by UNESCO in 1960 and went on to combat religious, racial, and other discrimination in public education. This was enforced so that public education protected what was constitutionally mandated. In the 1970's and 80's, the topic of sex education was being debated. What part was the parent's obligation and what was society's obligation came before Congress and the American public. What once only taught social hygiene was now to include more explicit information regarding sexually transmitted disease and unplanned pregnancy. In the early 1990's, public education evaluated the way students with disabilities were being accommodated in the average classroom. This outcry and investigation led to legislation protecting the rights of disabled Americans to benefit from free access to education. The bottom line is that public education and family values have been intertwined since the entity's inception.

Our post 9/11 world experienced a resurgence in patriotism. However, the practice of teaching our national identity has fallen behind the needs of worthy special interests that had not been specifically addressed when mandatory schooling was initiated. So now, as patriotism has been called on the proverbial carpet of our evening news, how do we promote what has historically been a cultural necessity?

The establishment of Constitution Day or Citizenship Day (September 17th) as a non-federal holiday in 1787 was added to the Congressional record in 1941 when Hungarian immigrant Clara Vajda sparked the idea to teach all citizens to appreciate the honor national sovereignty afford them. The Speaker of the House, Thad Wasielewski of Wisconsin, reported that the charity of a foreign-born citizen is ultimately responsible for the Act that should have embed the teaching of patriotism in every public school classroom.

Neither Vajda or Wasielewski had an inkling that the world would be discussing topics like gender more than we are our own national identities. Patriotism is no so easily defined nowadays because many

Americans choose to self-identify by their special interests above their citizenship. Occupations, sexual orientation, ethnicity, even religion, can separate us from what it used to mean to be patriotic when we only focus on difference. As Americans, we have to remember that it is our embraced differences that make us Americans, those differences we do not embrace destroy what it means to be American.

For educators welcoming a new class this month, teaching patriotism may have to be factored into what it means to teach embracing difference. Because if we make a decision to recognize and embrace difference, we can actually see we have more in common as Americans than we have incongruous. To illustrate it physically, when we literally embrace someone or something, we completely blur the line that separates us from that person or thing. We become one. Now that's a patriotic idea.

The Whisper Room

Mid-year elections are held every other November and are quickly becoming the hottest topic in town. As we recall the September 11th tragedy, it's nearly impossible to recall a pre-9/11 America. Everything has changed since that fateful day when nearly 3,000 lives were lost. Even though three presidents have bolstered the un-official national holiday marking America's greatest home front sacrifice since the Civil War, it has not been enough to bring this nation back together. In fact, since 9/11, the nation appears more fractured than it was before.

We have seen a Democrat in office as well as a Republican in the seventeen years that have passed. The question we must begin asking ourselves is "What are we doing differently, that actually makes a difference?" To begin to answer the question we need to get down to the bottom line of why people insist on pointing out every difference found in America foregoing the commonalities that make us one nation, under God.

The Whisper Room Series of politically inspired children's books paint a different picture anyone can understand. It depicts a return to the Constitutional principles that characterize America and the American people. These clear cut understandings use appropriate vocabulary to express the details and responsibilities September 11th rekindled for Americans on either side of the aisle.

With titles ranging from Patriot Day, commemorating and educating on the importance of recalling the events of September 11th, to Marshall's Ruling, that enforced the doctrine of judicial review, The Whisper Room Series gives an understandable explanation and call to action in favor of patriotism, unity, and education. These stories conclude with a Patriot's Creed and lesson on American symbolism - a fit foundation for any reader.

You can find The Whisper Room books on Amazon.

About the Author

Lisa Noël Babbage is an author, teacher, and philanthropist who has dedicated her keyboard to challenging topics that edify her readers. The great-granddaughter, four times removed, of English polymath Charles Babbage, she has spent seventeen years teaching math and science in the public school system in Georgia, where she lives. In 2011, she took a three-year leave of absence from her profession to inaugurate a non-profit organization, Maranatha House Ministries (MHM, Inc.), aimed at the fight against homelessness. After a childhood spent in and out of homeless shelters herself, Lisa is committed to helping families stay off the streets of American cities.

https://lisanoelbabbage.com

Also by Lisa Babbage

Books by Lisa Noel Babbage span from academic memoir, early learner, devotional, to religious companion texts. Through her self publishing arm, Botany Bay Books, she has published and released over twenty-five titles and continues to write for all audiences. Her books can be purchased on Amazon.com as well as fine retailers everywhere.

333 Miracles A testimony of Continued Blessings

To varying degrees, life can be overwhelming. For many, it seems as though problems pile up on one another with no end in sight. A cycle of lack and defeat makes hope seem like an unreachable concept. Lisa Noël Babbage shows people that there is hope. In 333 Miracles, she shares her personal story, one that is marked by traumas such as sexual and drug abuse, divorce, and cancer. Her testimony recalls more than thirty years of bondage which was brought to an end by the path she walked with Jesus Christ. She identifies biblical principles learned on her journey to hope relating experiences that speak to all people. Her openness about her experiences help readers learn how a closer relationship with God can help you reach beyond trauma to find hope.

333 Miracles introduces people and relates experiences that can speak to anyone. Babbage's openness about her experiences help readers learn how a closer relationship to God can help them reach beyond the traumas to find hope.

Not So Cookie Cutter Kids

Not So Cookie Cutter Kids chronicles Lisa Noël Babbage's the last year of public school teaching using self reflections as a professional practice by which she identified strategies for coping

215

with twenty-five student characteristics. For teachers, coaches, parents, and school administrators, Not So Cookie Cutter Kids is a hybrid, a new genre that is part academic and part biographical. This academic memoir argues the basis for statistically infused self reflection, when used with in the Teacher's Edition Bundle, to improve student performance and reduce teacher burnout.

Made in the USA
Middletown, DE
19 June 2022